"A Welcome Ad

"Someone has said, 'A ... at the mercy of a man with a paradigm based on good and necessary consequences.' Greg Gibson's new book *All Old Testament Laws Cancelled* is not a new paradigm deduced from a new set of hermeneutics, it's a collection of Scripture texts piled one on top of another. It is written in the style of J.C. Ryle. The book has extremely well chosen quotations. It is a welcome addition to the growing number of books on New Covenant Theology. I personally think the author does not make a sharp enough distinction between the Old Covenant and the Old Testament. I would title the book *All Old Covenant Laws Cancelled*." John Reisinger, Author of *Tablets of Stone*

"*ALL* Old Testament Laws Cancelled"

24 Reasons Why All Old Testament Laws Are Cancelled
And All New Testament Laws Are for Our Obedience

Greg Gibson

Dedicated to all who base their practice on
Old Testament laws, including:

Reformed, Covenant Theologians;
Seventh-Day Adventists;
Other Sabbath-Keepers;
And Roman Catholics

JesusSaidFollowMe Publishing
www.JesusSaidFollowMe.org

Printed in the United States of America

Library of Congress Cataloging-in-Publication Data

Gibson, Greg.
    All old testament laws cancelled : 24 reasons why all old testament laws are cancelled and all new testament laws are for our obedience / Greg Gibson.
    Includes bibliography and index.
    ISBN 978-971-94222-0-4
    1. Christianity / Calvinist.
    2. Christian Theology / Ethics.
    3. Christianity / Seventh-Day Adventist.
    I. Title

BV1-5099 (Practical Theology)

Abridged Table of Contents

See the *Expanded Table of Contents* on the next page...

Expanded Table of Contents

Author's Preface

When I was an "omniscient teenager," I decided to read through the whole Bible, starting from the Old Testament. Soon, I stopped eating pork, and started keeping the Sabbath. Later, I wondered if I'd go to hell if I stopped keeping the Sabbath. Now, I know I wasn't the only one confused.

Also, when I was a one-year old babe in Christ, my Presbyterian friends tried to convince me of infant baptism, while my Baptist friends tried to convince me of believer's baptism. However, I didn't understand then that Reformed, Covenant Theology's infant baptism was a practice based on the Old Testament command for Abraham to circumcise all the males (infants and adults) in his household.

> "It is true that there is no express command to baptize infants in the New Testament, no express record of the baptism of infants, and no passages so stringently implying it that we must infer from them that infants were baptized...the warrant for infant baptism is not to be sought in the New Testament but in the Old Testament, when the Church was instituted..."[1]

Christians have debated this law controversy since the 1st century:

- Pharisee believers vs. Gentile believers (1st century, Acts 15)
- Roman Empire Church vs. "Anabaptists" (4th - 16th centuries)
- Reformers vs. Anabaptists (16th century Reformation)

Perhaps the Bible's 3 most complex, theological questions are:

- God's sovereignty and man's will?
- The Law in the New Testament?
- End time prophecy?

"...Jonathan Edwards (1703-58) observed, 'There is perhaps no part of divinity attended with so much intricacy, and wherein

---

[1] B.B. Warfield, *Studies in Theology*, 399-400, in "Warfield on the Warrant for Infant Baptism," Midwest Center for Theological Studies Blog, http://www.mctsowensboro.org/blog/?p=365, Rich Barcellos, May 6, 2008.

orthodox divines…differ as stating the precise agreement and difference between the 2 dispensations of Moses and Christ.'"[2]

As I read different views on the law, I'm amazed at how much fuzzy thinking exists. What I've tried to do here is clear up some of that fog.

My thesis is simple: All Old Testament laws are cancelled, and all New Testament laws are for our obedience. But, you don't have to agree with me to fellowship with me. If you know and love the Lord Jesus Christ, that's good enough for me.

New Covenant Theology (the view in this book) is a rapidly-spreading view with a better priest, better sacrifice, and better covenant (containing a better law).

Jesus prayed for us, "…May they be brought to complete unity to let the world know that you sent Me…" (Jn. 17:23, NIV). May it please the Father to answer His Son's prayer, even through this book.

"The New Covenant Reformation"

1. Scripture Alone: Our authority is the Bible alone, not tradition.

2. Grace Alone: God saves us by His grace alone, not our works.

3. Faith Alone: God justifies us by faith alone, not our works.

4. Christ Alone: Salvation is by Christ alone, not priests, saints, etc.

5. Glory to God Alone: Bible preaching and Christian living are God-centered alone, not man-centered.

6. Regeneration Alone: The New Covenant Church includes the regenerate alone, not the unregenerate (baptized infants, or all who prayed a "sinner's prayer" but prove to be hypocrites or apostates).

7. New Covenant Alone: New Covenant Christians obey all New Testament laws alone, not Old Testament laws (the Sabbath, food laws, infant baptism, priesthood, and state-church theocracy).

---

[2] Stanley N. Gundry, Ed., *Five Views on Law and Gospel*, (Grand Rapids: Eerdmans, 14).

Introduction

Have you ever felt confused trying to understand what the New Testament teaches about the law? Ever struggled with how to interpret Paul's apparent contradictory, positive and negative statements about the law? Is the law good or bad? Ever wondered which commands God will hold you accountable for on the Judgment Day? For example...

- If you work on the Sabbath, will you go to hell?
- Is it still a sin to eat pork bacon, sausage, or hot dogs?
- Should we baptize believers only, or also their infants?
- Do we need human priests to represent us before God?
- Should the government execute adulterers and gays?

Or, since we're "not under the law"...

- What is sin?
- How can you know right from wrong?
- Do we have defined, objective, specific laws?

Every Spirit-born heart cries out, "Lord, what do you want me to do? How can I please you?" (1 Cor. 7:32; 1 Thes. 4:1).

Let's be honest, few issues in the New Testament are harder to understand than the law. (I confess that I still have some questions.) Many sincere brothers differ about the law.

The goal of this study is to help you harmonize all (not merely some) of the Bible's verses on law, so that you will obey all that Christ commanded. Here are the 5 main conclusions you'll see below...

1. The whole Old Testament is still useful for doctrine/faith.
2. All Old Testament commands were cancelled.
3. Some Old Testament commands were transferred to the N.T.
4. All New Testament commands are for our obedience.
5. Our obedience is often motivated by truths about Christ.

If it can be proven that all Old Testament commands are cancelled, then that undermines the foundation of all Old Covenant - based groups including Roman Catholicism; Mormonism; Adventism; Reformed, Covenant Theology; etc. (Among those 4 major groups, the only evangelical one is Covenant Theology.)

Here are 6 popular views of which commands we must obey…

6 Popular Views on Which Laws We Must Obey	
Orthodox Judaism	<ins>All O.T., and No N.T. Laws:</ins> 1. Decalogue 2. Temple 3. Priests, sacrifices 4. State-Church theocracy 5. Infant members
Roman Catholicism	<ins>Some O.T., and All N.T. Laws:</ins> 1. Decalogue 2. Priests, sacrifices 3. State-Church theocracy 4. Infant members 5. All N.T. laws
Theocracy, Reformed, Covenant Theology	<ins>Some O.T., and All N.T. Laws:</ins> 1. Decalogue 2. State-Church theocracy 3. Infant members 4. All N.T. laws
Non-Theocracy, Reformed, Covenant Theology	<ins>Some O.T., and All N.T. Laws:</ins> 1. Decalogue 2. Infant members 3. All N.T. laws
Reformed Baptist, Covenant Theology	<ins>Some O.T., and All N.T. Laws:</ins> 1. Decalogue 2. All N.T. laws
New Covenant Theology	<ins>No O.T., and All N.T. Laws:</ins> 1. All N.T. laws
Antinomianism	<ins>No O.T., and No N.T. Laws:</ins> 0. No laws

Only 3 of the above views use consistent O.T. - N.T. hermeneutics: Orthodox Judaism, New Covenant Theology, and Antinomianism. The other 4 views mix inconsistent, selective O.T. - N.T. hermeneutics.

Before We Start...

Portray: The theological labels below are intended to portray only some, not all, who profess them. Within most labels, you'll find diversity, not uniformity. The goal of the 20 charts is to illustrate only some popular views, not all historical or scholarly views. (So, if the shoe fits, wear it.)

Obey: The Bible is Christ-centered. Preaching is Christ-centered. And, sanctification is Christ-centered. Yet, it's OK to focus temporarily on law for the purposes of debate, definition, and topical study. This book is not designed as a comprehensive, balanced study on preaching or sanctification. (Those topics would require whole books!) This book focuses mostly on only one part of our sanctification: Obeying God's commands. The focus is more on which commands to obey (N.T.), rather than how to obey (the Holy Spirit's grace), or why to obey (love).

Pray: We learn more when we humble ourselves to pray for wisdom. If we would pray before reading anything, then we would agree more because the same Spirit would teach us the same truth. Will you please consider praying, "Lord, if I'm right, please don't let me be deceived. But if I'm wrong, please correct me now, instead of on the Judgment Day?" I've prayed that prayer many times, and I hope you will too.

Thesis: All Old Testament Laws Are Cancelled, And All New Testament Laws Are for Our Obedience

The thesis I'm going to try to prove here is simply this: "All Old Testament commands are cancelled, and all New Testament commands are for our obedience." (O.T. laws are cancelled for regulation, but not revelation.) So, what is the history of this view?

Most of the Apostolic Fathers were non-Sabbatarians (but I don't know their views on other Old Testament laws).

And, many of the "Anabaptists" from the 4th - 16th centuries based their practice on the New Testament. The 16th-century Anabaptists were especially clear on this...

> "...the Anabaptists, their view of the law was relatively monolithic (Munsterites excepted). They are widely recognized for their insistence on the newness of the New Covenant. For the Radical Reformers, the law which Christ spoke was no mere reissuing of Sinai. It marked a significant shift in God's program...they emphatically taught that the distinction between the OT and the NT is absolute, and it is the NT alone that is normative in questions of Christian ethics. (cf. Estep, *The Anabaptist Story*, 142-144) Christ's fulfillment of Moses' law is precisely what rendered it 'old.' It is not merely part of the old law that is abolished; it is the whole of it that is fulfilled and so displaced by the new. The idea here is not so much that of 'advance' as it is change."[3]

Among today's scholars, Doug Moo sounds like he shares some similarities to my thesis...

> "I will state at this point the position for which I will argue: The entire Mosaic law comes to fulfillment in Christ, and this fulfillment means that this law is no longer a *direct and immediate* source of, or judge of, the conduct of God's people. Christian behavior, rather, is now guided directly by 'the law of Christ.' This 'law' does not consist of legal prescriptions and ordinances, but of the teaching and example of Jesus and the apostles, the central demand of love, and the guiding influence of the indwelling Holy Spirit."[4]

And, Nathan Busenitz (John MacArthur's assistant) of *Shepherds' Fellowship* wrote a series on the law with some common ground...

---

[3] Tom Wells and Fred Zaspel, *New Covenant Theology*, (Frederick, MD: New Covenant Media, 2002), 83.
[4] Douglas J. Moo, "The Law of Christ as the Fulfillment of the Law of Moses," in Gundry, 343.

"...how are Christians practically to approach the Old Testament Law? Clearly, they are not to follow all of its restrictions, for the Law of Christ has replaced the Law of Moses...First, believers must recognize that the Mosaic Law is not binding for Christians. This includes all of the individual precepts that make up that Law. These commands, whether deemed moral, ceremonial, or civil, were part of God's covenant with Israel. They are not part of His covenant with the Church."[5]

Discontinuity in Practice, But Continuity in Doctrine

For centuries, theologians have debated how much continuity vs. discontinuity exists between the Old Testament and the New Testament. In this book, I'll try to show that the simple answer is there is discontinuity in practice, but continuity in doctrine/faith.

There is discontinuity in practice between the Old Testament vs. the New Testament since they contain 2 separate laws (although many of the same commands are transferred). And, there is continuity in doctrine/faith between them since God never changes. (Also, there is continuity in God's one, eternal plan in Christ which organizes all the covenants and the whole Bible.)

Are O.T. Laws Continued if Not Cancelled, Or Cancelled if Not Repeated?

One of the reasons why many disagree on this question about law is because they start with opposite hermeneutics. Those who defend obeying some Old Testament laws often assume that all Old Testament laws are continued unless they're cancelled in the New Testament. While those who defend obeying only New Testament laws, often assume that all Old Testament laws are cancelled if they're not repeated in the New Testament. (Personally, I view Old Testament laws repeated in the New Testament as transferred, instead of continued.)

---

[5] Nathan Busenitz, "Wrapping Up the Law," *Pulpit Magazine*, (Shepherds' Fellowship: 2/28/08), www.sfpulpit.com/2008/02/28/wrapping-up-the-law/

If all Old Testament laws were cancelled, how would you expect God to say it? Of course, you wouldn't expect Him to have to cancel all 613 laws individually in the New Testament. Wouldn't it be more likely to expect Him to say that the (whole) law is cancelled? As you'll see below, He's said many times and in many ways that the (whole) law and (whole) Old Covenant are "cancelled."

"The 30-Second, Law-View Test"

Here's a simple test to identify anyone's law hermeneutic in less than 30 seconds. If a Christian child dishonors his parents, which command did he violate?

1. Both Ex. 20:12 and Eph. 6:2 (Covenant Theology).
2. Neither Ex. 20:12 nor Eph. 6:2 (Antinomianism).
3. Only Eph. 6:2, not Ex. 20:12 (New Covenant Theology).

This test will instantly and clearly define anyone's view of God's law.

Now, let's take those same, 3 systems above and try to diagram them. Look closely at the 3, following diagrams. If you can understand these diagrams, then you will understand this whole book...

3 Different Views of the Law of God
Throughout Redemptive History

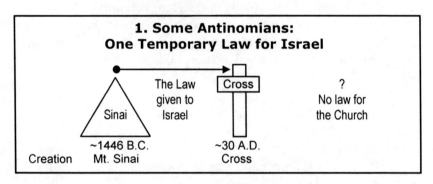

1. Some Antinomians:
One Temporary Law for Israel

The Law given to Israel — Sinai

Cross

?
No law for the Church

~1446 B.C. Mt. Sinai
Creation

~30 A.D. Cross

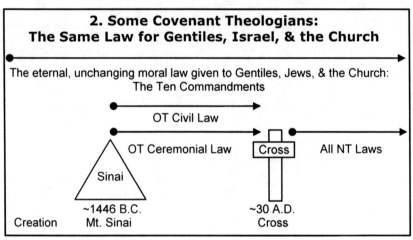

2. Some Covenant Theologians:
The Same Law for Gentiles, Israel, & the Church

The eternal, unchanging moral law given to Gentiles, Jews, & the Church: The Ten Commandments

OT Civil Law

OT Ceremonial Law

Sinai

Cross

All NT Laws

Creation
~1446 B.C. Mt. Sinai

~30 A.D. Cross

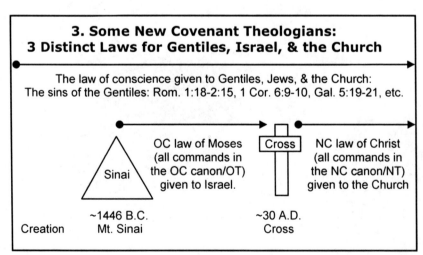

3. Some New Covenant Theologians:
3 Distinct Laws for Gentiles, Israel, & the Church

The law of conscience given to Gentiles, Jews, & the Church:
The sins of the Gentiles: Rom. 1:18-2:15, 1 Cor. 6:9-10, Gal. 5:19-21, etc.

Sinai

OC law of Moses
(all commands in
the OC canon/OT)
given to Israel.

Cross

NC law of Christ
(all commands in
the NC canon/NT)
given to the Church

~1446 B.C. Mt. Sinai
Creation

~30 A.D. Cross

Universal law is revealed in the conscience. And, some of that conscience law is also revealed in covenant law. So, for sins revealed in both, there is overlap. For example, if Gentiles, Jews, or Christians committed adultery, which laws did they violate?

1. Gentiles violate only the law of conscience, not Ex. 20:14; Rom. 1:24; etc.

2. Old Covenant Jews violate the law of conscience and O.C. law from Ex. 20:14; etc.

3. New Covenant saints violate the law of conscience and N.C. law from Rom. 1:24; etc.

"The 5 P's of Obedience"

1. The Picture of obedience: The Lord Jesus Christ (who we obey).

2. The Power for Obedience: The Holy Spirit's effectual grace (how we obey).

3. The Position of Obedience: In Christ/union with Him (where we obey from; "Since you are…, therefore obey" not "If you obey, then you will become…").

4. The Prompts for Obedience: Indicative/doctrinal truths in the O.T. – N.T. (why we obey).

5. The Practice of Obedience: All New Testament commands (what we obey).

As I mentioned earlier, this book defines and defends #5, what we obey.

So much for the introduction. Are you ready now to search the Scriptures? OK, here are 9 objections to, "All Old Testament laws are cancelled."

Part I.
9 Objections to "All Old Testament Laws Are Cancelled"

The following 9 objections are popular among some Covenant Theologians, Seventh Day Adventists, Messianic Jews, and other Sabbath-keeping groups. Since Covenant Theology (held by many Calvinists) is the most influential view, we will focus on it.

1. "But the Ten Commandments Are the Eternal, Unchanging, Moral Law of God"

First of all, you're right that God probably has one eternal, unchanging, so-called "moral law" for all people of all times. Even though it isn't explicitly stated in Scripture, we can imply it from 3 facts…

> 1. Guilty consciences of all humans, including Gentile heathen (Rom. 1:18-32ff.)

> 2. Providential judgment of all humans, including Gentile heathen (the Flood, Egypt's plagues, Sodom, etc.)

> 3. The final judgment of all humans, including Gentile heathen (1 Cor. 6:9-10; Gal. 5:19-21; Rev. 21:8, etc.)

The fact that all humans have a conscience implies they know specific acts are right or wrong (sin). The fact that God providentially judged some unbelievers like Sodom and Gomorrah (Gen. 19) and Herod (Acts 12:22-23) implies that He has a standard of right and wrong (sin). And, the fact that God will judge all men in the end implies that He will do so by a standard of right and wrong (sin).

Whether those 3 examples of law are the same, and eternal and unchanging, we don't know for sure, but it's highly likely. Yet, the term "moral law" is confusing. Perhaps a better term is "conscience law."

Second, the real question is, "Where are those standards defined in Scripture: The Ten Commandments, or elsewhere?" Is there anywhere in Scripture that defines the sins of all humans (Gentiles, Israel, and the Church) for all times? On the Judgment Day, what standard will God use to judge Gentile heathen: The Decalogue or another standard?

Yes, there are several, major passages that define the sins of all humans (including Gentiles) for all times: The sin lists for all humans are the most likely definition of the so-called "moral law of God"…

"You shall not do as they do in the land of Egypt, where you lived, and you shall not do as they do in the land of Canaan, to which I am bringing you...None of you shall approach any one of his close relatives to uncover nakedness...You shall not approach a woman to uncover her nakedness while she is in her menstrual uncleanness. And you shall not lie sexually with your neighbor's wife and so make yourself unclean with her. You shall not give any of your children to offer them to Molech, and so profane the name of your God: I am the LORD. You shall not lie with a male as with a woman; it is an abomination. And you shall not lie with any animal...Do not make yourselves unclean by any of these things, for by all these the nations I am driving out before you have become unclean..." (Lev. 18:1-30).

The sins of the Gentiles here include incest, menstrual sex, adultery, child sacrifice, homosexuality, and beastiality. (Perhaps God revealed incest as conscience law after Adam's early descendants married, later in Genesis.) And, Leviticus 18 reveals the same laws that God probably revealed to the conscience. (But, since all Old Testament laws are cancelled, if a man commits incest today, he violated the law of conscience, not Leviticus 18, which still tells us what is probably written on the conscience.)

"For the wrath of God is revealed from heaven against all ungodliness and unrighteousness of men...idolatry, lusts, impurity, lesbianism, homosexuality, unrighteousness, evil, covetousness, malice, envy, murder, strife, deceit, maliciousness, gossips, slanderers, haters of God, insolent, haughty, boastful, inventors of evil, disobedient to parents, foolish, faithless, heartless, ruthless. Though they know God's decree that those who practice such things deserve to die..." (Rom. 1:18-32).

"Do you not know that the unrighteous will not inherit the kingdom of God? Do not be deceived: neither the sexually immoral, nor idolaters, nor adulterers, nor men who practice homosexuality, nor thieves, nor the greedy, nor drunkards, nor revilers, nor swindlers will inherit the kingdom of God" (1 Cor. 6:9-10).

"Now the works of the flesh are evident: sexual immorality, impurity, sensuality, idolatry, sorcery, enmity, strife, jealousy, fits of anger, rivalries, dissensions, divisions, envy, drunkenness, orgies, and things like these. I warn you, as I warned you before, that those who do such things will not inherit the kingdom of God" (Gal. 5:19-21).

"But as for the cowardly, the faithless, the detestable, as for murderers, the sexually immoral, sorcerers, idolaters, and all liars, their portion will be in the lake that burns with fire and sulfur which is the second death" (Rev. 21:8).

"Outside are the dogs and sorcerers and the sexually immoral and murderers and idolaters, and everyone who loves and practices falsehood" (Rev. 22:15).

Also, for those Jews who heard Christ in the 1st century, the standard of judgment will be Christ's words...

"the word that I have spoken will judge him on the last day" (Jn. 12:48).

The Holy Spirit says that the sins of all men (including Gentiles) are defined in Lev. 18; Rom. 1; 1 Cor. 6:9-10; Gal. 5:19-21; Rev. 21:8, 22:15; etc. (never the Ten Commandments). The texts do not say these are the only sins of the Gentiles. These are not exhaustive lists.

> **"The Holy Spirit says that the sins of the Gentiles are defined in Rom. 1; Rev. 21:8, 22:15; etc. (never the Ten Commandments)."**

Interestingly, in Romans 1, God lists 30 sins, but not the Sabbath. The absence of the Sabbath from those 6, Gentile sin lists above is significant.

Not only has God never said that the sins of the Gentiles are defined in the Ten Commandments, He even says that Gentiles do not have the law...

"The LORD our God made a covenant (a.k.a. "The Ten Commandments") with us in Horeb. *Not with our fathers did the LORD make this covenant (Ten Commandments)*, but with us..." (Deut. 5:2-3).

"He declares His word to Jacob, His statutes and rules to Israel, *He has not dealt thus with any other nation; they do not know His rules"* (Ps. 147:19-20).

"For all who have sinned *without the law* will also perish *without the law...Gentiles, who do not have the law..."* (Rom. 2:12-14).

"To *those outside the law I became as one outside the law...*that I might win *those outside the law"* (1 Cor. 9:21).

When you read the phrase "the law" it's important to understand that the Ten Commandments were the foundational document of the whole law. So, when God says that the Gentiles do not have the law, He means the whole Decalogue and all the other Old Covenant commands. (Although, they had *some* of the same laws in their conscience which God also recorded in the Decalogue.)

So, the eternal, unchanging law for all men at all times is revealed in the sin lists for all men, not the Decalogue in Exodus 20. (By the way, no Gentile heathen or convert has ever testified to knowing about the Sabbath. Therefore, there is no evidence that God has ever written the whole Decalogue on their hearts.)

What about the fact that the Ten Commandments are distinguished from the rest of the law? Granted, the Ten Commandments are distinguished from the law, but never divorced from the law.

> **"Granted, the Ten Commandments are distinguished from the law, but never divorced from the law."**

But, why did God distinguish the Ten Commandments from the rest of the law? Because they are the Old Covenant's foundational document, not the eternal, unchanging, moral law of God.

The Ten Commandments = the Old Covenant (Document)

"…And He wrote on the tablets the words of *the covenant, the Ten Commandments"* (Ex. 34:28).

"And He declared to you *His covenant* which He commanded you to perform, that is, *the Ten Commandments…* " (Deut. 4:13).

"…the ark, in which is the covenant (Ten Commandments) of the LORD that He made with our fathers, when He brought them out of the land of Egypt" (1 Kings 8:21).

"…the ark, in which is the covenant (Ten Commandments) of the LORD that He made with the people of Israel" (2 Chr. 6:11).

Could anything be clearer? God uses the phrases "Old Covenant" and "Ten Commandments" almost synonymously. (Although, the Ten Commandments represent the whole Old Covenant, they are not the whole covenant. The Ten Commandments are the foundation document on which the rest of the Old Covenant is built.)

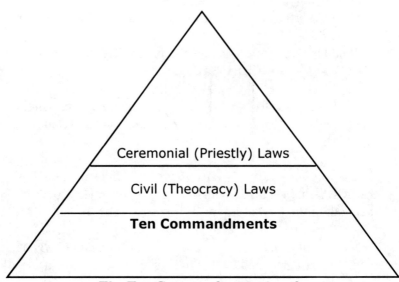

The Ten Commandments Are the
Foundation Document of the Whole Old Covenant

So, when you hear the phrase "Ten Commandments," God wants you to think, "the Old Covenant." Here are the other 11 ideas you should think when hearing the name "Ten Commandments"...

The 12 Names for the Decalogue in All 56 Verses:
"Ten Commandments" Only 3 Times (Zero in the N.T.)

When you hear the words, "Ten Commandments," what's the first thought that comes to your mind? If you automatically think, "The moral law of God," then your view is very different from God's view.

Depending on how you classify them, the whole Decalogue and its synonyms appear ~56 times in Scripture. (We'll exclude the names "ark of the covenant," "ark of the testimony," and "tabernacle of the testimony," even though they would be accurate.) And, in those 56 occurrences, God calls the Decalogue by 12 different names. Listed below, are the number of times He uses each name.

Old Testament:
14 = The tablets (Ex. 32:15, 32:16a,b, 32:19, 34:1b,c, 34:28;
      Deut. 9:17, 10:2a,b, 10:3, 10:4, 10:5; 2 Chr. 5:10)
13 = The tablets of stone (Ex. 24:12, 31:18, 34:1, 34:4a,b;
      Deut. 4:13, 5:22, 9:9, 9:10, 9:11, 10:1, 10:3; 1 Kg. 8:9)
10 = The testimony (Ex. 16:34, 25:16, 25:21, 27:21, 30:6, 30:36,
      40:20; Lev. 16:13; Num 17:4, 17:10)
 3 = The tablets of the testimony (Ex. 31:18, 32:15, 34:29)
 3 = The tablets of the covenant (Deut. 9:9, 9:11, 9:15)
 3 = The Ten Commandments (Ex. 34:28; Deut. 4:13; 10:4)
 2 = The covenant (1 Kg. 8:21; 2 Chr. 6:11)
 1 = The words of the covenant (Ex 34:28)
 1 = His covenant (Deut. 4:13)
 0 = The moral law

New Testament:
 2 = The letter (2 Cor. 3:6a,b)
 1 = Letters on stone (2 Cor. 3:7)
 1 = Tablets of stone (2 Cor. 3:3)
 1 = The handwriting of ordinances (Col. 2:14)
 1 = The tablets of the covenant (Heb. 9:4)
 0 = The Ten Commandments
 0 = The moral law

So, when you hear the phrase "the Ten Commandments," the first thought that should come to your mind is, "tablets (of stone"), not "moral law." Remember, another thought that should come to your mind is "the covenant."

Do you think of the Ten Commandments as "the tablets of stone," and "the covenant" (Old Covenant made with Israel?) When talking about the Ten Commandments, if you have to *rely* on words uninspired by the Holy Spirit (like "moral law") to explain your theology, then you probably have a different theology than the Holy Spirit.

> **"...if you have to *rely* on words uninspired by the Holy Spirit (like "moral law") to explain your theology, then you probably have a different theology than the Holy Spirit."**

Did you see how many times the phrase "Ten Commandments" appears in the New Testament? Zero! (Think about that.)

**Everything the N.T. Says About The Whole Decalogue:
Only 3 Passages, All Negative**

As we saw above, the Holy Spirit never uses the names "Ten Commandments" or "moral law" in the New Testament. As a matter of fact, there are only 3 New Testament passages that definitely refer to the whole Decalogue, and they're all negative…

1. "The letter," "letters on stone," and "tablets of stone" (2 Cor. 3:6-9) are:

- Not where the Spirit writes (2 Cor. 3:3)
- (What) kills (2 Cor. 3:6)
- A ministry of death (2 Cor. 3:7)
- A ministry of condemnation (2 Cor. 3:9)

2. "The handwriting of ordinances" (Col. 2:14) was:

- Blotted out (Col. 2:14)
- Taken away (Col. 2:14)
- Nailed to the cross (Col. 2:14)

3. "The tablets of the covenant" (Heb. 9:4) are:

- Obsolete (Heb. 8:13)
- Growing old (Heb. 8:13)
- Ready to vanish." (Heb. 8:13)

But, why did God combine 9 universal laws of conscience from the Gentiles with one symbolic law (the Sabbath) in the Ten Commandments? And, why did He include only 9 of the Ten Commandments in the law of Christ for the Church?

The answer is simple. Archaeology reveals that God designed the Old Covenant with some similarities to ancient, near-eastern treaties. And in those treaties, the sign of the covenant was placed in the middle of the covenant document. Likewise, the Sabbath was the sign of the covenant, placed in the middle of the Old Covenant document, the Decalogue…

"As a further detail in the parallelism of external appearance it is tempting to see in *the Sabbath sign presented in the midst of the ten words the equivalent of the suzerain's dynastic seal found in the midst of the obverse of the international treaty documents*…the Sabbath is declared to be his 'sign of the covenant' (Ex. 31:13-17)."[6]

The Sabbath Was the Sign of the Old Covenant

Do you know what the sign was of Moses' covenant?

"…Above all, you shall *keep my Sabbaths, for this is a sign* between Me and you…Therefore the people of Israel shall keep the Sabbath, observing the Sabbath throughout their generations *as a covenant* forever. *It is a sign* forever between Me and the people of Israel…" (Ex. 31:13-17).

"Moreover, I gave them my *Sabbaths, as a sign* between me and them…" (Ezek. 20:12).

"…keep my Sabbaths holy that they may be a *sign* between me and you…" (Ezek. 20:20).

The Sabbath was the sign of the Old Covenant. Therefore, if you keep the Sabbath sign, you're SIGN(ifying) that you're under the Old Covenant, law of Moses. If the Abrahamic Covenant was "the covenant of circumcision" (Acts 7:8), then the Old Covenant was the "covenant of Sabbath."

---

[6] Meredith Kline, *The Structure of Biblical Authority,* 2nd Edition, (Grand Rapids: Eerdmans, 1975), 120.

The Signs of the Covenants	
The Sign of Noah's Covenant: Rainbow	"This is the *sign of the covenant*... I have set My bow in the cloud, and it shall be a *sign of the covenant*... This is the *sign of the covenant*... "* (Gen. 9:12-17).
The Sign of Abraham's Covenant: Circumcision	"This *IS my covenant*...Every male among you shall be circumcised...it shall be a sign of the covenant..." (Gen. 17:10-11). "And He gave him *the covenant of circumcision...*" (Acts 7:8).
The Sign of Moses' Covenant: Sabbath	"...keep my Sabbaths, for this is a sign between me and you... observing the Sabbath throughout their generations *as a covenant* forever. It is a sign..." (Ex. 31:13, 16, 17; Ezek. 20:12, 20).
The Sign of Christ's Covenant: Lord's Supper	"...This is My body...This cup that is poured out for you *IS the New Covenant...*" (Lk. 22:19-20; cf. Gen. 17:10).

But, doesn't the Bible say that the Sabbath is forever? Yes, and so are circumcision, the Passover, and the Day of Atonement. So, how can we harmonize these "eternal" commands with the New Testament cancelling them?

Here's a solution: The Old Testament physical laws are cancelled, but their spiritual symbolism is fulfilled eternally in Christ.

Eternal Laws Fulfilled Eternally in Christ	
Circumcision Is Everlasting: "...shall surely be circumcised. So shall my covenant be in your flesh an everlasting covenant" (Gen. 17:13).	**Regeneration Is Circumcision (Forever):** "...nor is circumcision outward and physical. But a Jew is one inwardly, and circumcision is a matter of the heart, by the Spirit..." (Rom. 2:28-29). "For neither circumcision counts for anything, nor uncircumcision, but a new creation" (Gal. 6:15). "In Him also you were circumcised with a circumcision made without hands, by putting off the body of the flesh, by the circumcision of Christ" (Col. 2:11; cf. Rom. 2:28-29; 1 Cor. 7:18-19; Gal. 5:2-3, 6; Phil. 3:3).
The Passover Is Forever: "This day shall be for you a memorial day, and you shall keep it as a feast to the LORD; throughout your generations, as a statute forever, you shall keep it as a feast" (Ex. 12:14).	**Christ Is Our Passover (Forever):** "...For Christ, our Passover lamb, has been sacrificed. Let us therefore celebrate the festival, not with the old leaven, the leaven of malice and evil, but with the unleavened bread of sincerity & truth" (1 Cor. 5:7-8).
The Day of Atonement Is Forever: "And this shall be a statute forever for you, that atonement may be made for the people of Israel once in the year because of all their sins" (Lev. 16:34,	**Christ Atoned Eternally:** "...the priests go regularly into the first section, performing their ritual duties, but into the second only the high priest goes, and he but once a year...But when Christ appeared as a high

cf. 16:29, 31).	priest...he entered once for all into the holy places...thus securing an *eternal* redemption" (Heb. 9:6-12).
The Sabbath Is Forever: "Therefore the people of Israel shall keep the Sabbath, observing the Sabbath throughout their generations, a covenant forever" (Ex. 31:16).	**Christ Is Our Sabbath Rest (Forever):** "Therefore let no one pass judgment on you in questions of food and drink, or with regard to a festival or a new moon or a Sabbath. These are a shadow of the things to come, but the substance belongs to Christ" (Col. 2:16-17). "For we who have believed enter that rest...for whoever has entered God's rest has also rested from his works as God did from his" (Heb. 4:3, 9-10; cf. Rom. 14:5-6; Gal. 4:9-11).

In other words, Christ is our eternal atonement and Passover because He sacrificed Himself for our sins once for all time. And, we are eternally circumcised (regenerated) because we have received eternal life. And, we are eternally keeping Sabbath because we have entered into God's eternal rest by faith in Christ.

There is no explicit, Biblical evidence that the Ten Commandments are the eternal, unchanging, moral law of God. However, there are several, explicit passages defining the sins of all humans, including the Gentiles. And, there are 4 verses where God explicitly states that the Ten Commandments are the covenant. It's safer to build our doctrine on explicit exegesis, than implicit reasoning.

On the Judgment Day, can you imagine God condemning Gentile heathen to hell for Sabbath-breaking? They would ask, "What's the Sabbath?" That's why the Sabbath is missing from the Gentile sin lists.

7 Clear Facts About the Sabbath

1. Gentile Heathen and Converts Have Never Testified to Knowing About the Sabbath Written on Their Hearts

It's a fact, no Gentile heathen has ever testified to knowing about the Sabbath on his conscience. And, no Gentile heathen convert has ever testified to knowing about the Sabbath on his heart from regeneration. There's no evidence that God has ever written the *whole* Decalogue on any human heart from creation, or from regeneration.

These 2 unquestionable facts alone should be enough to end all debate about whether the Sabbath and the whole Decalogue are universal laws for Gentiles. The theory that the Sabbath is written on the heart has as much evidence as evolution.

2. Genesis 2:2-3 Is a Description, Not a Prescription

Genesis 2:2-3 is a creation description, not a prescription, or creation ordinance (command). God created, God blessed, and God rested, period! Adam didn't create, Adam didn't bless, and Adam didn't rest from creating. Adam could not have rested from creating because he didn't create.

There's no more evidence that Adam rested from creating than did the angels, animals, or serpent. Plus, the 7th day was only Adam's 2nd day. (Although, Adam didn't rest for 24 hours, but he may have entered into God's eternal rest.)

Contrary to popular Sabbatarian belief, Exodus 20:11 does not necessarily make God's creation rest in Genesis 2:2-3 our motive for keeping the Sabbath.

> "Remember the Sabbath day, to keep it holy...For in six days the LORD made the heaven and earth, the sea, and all that is in them, and rested the seventh day..." (Ex. 20:8, 11).

Was God's creation rest Israel's *motive* or *model* for keeping the Sabbath? More likely, it was their model since the Lord gave them a different motive (redemption from Egypt) in Deuteronomy 5:15.

"You shall remember that you were a slave in the land of Egypt, and the LORD your God brought you out from there with a mighty hand and an outstretched arm. Therefore the LORD your God commanded you to keep the Sabbath day" (Deut. 5:15).

3. Gen. 2:2-3 Is God's Eternal Rest, Not Man's 24-Hour, Weekly Rest

"...His works were finished from the foundation of the world" (Heb. 4:3c).

Since God ceased from creating, His rest was eternal, not 24 hours. He didn't start re-creating on the 8th day. And, obviously He didn't rest again every 7th day (the 14th day, 21st day, etc.) from His work of creating. In other words, this is God's eternal rest (Heb. 4:3, 11), not the 24-hour, weekly Sabbath rest given later in Exodus.

The Sabbath has 2 functions in redemptive history...

1. Eternal rest before the Fall, and by faith in Christ after the Fall (Gen. 2:2-3; Col. 2:16-17; Heb. 4:3, 11).

2. The Old Covenant sign/shadow of eschatological, eternal rest by faith in Christ (Ex. 31:13-17; Col. 2:16-17).

Beware of confusing the mere sign/shadow in Exodus 20 with the reality in Genesis 2. God created the human Sabbath in Exodus 16 to testify to His divine rest in Genesis 2, and coming in Christ.

4. God Introduced the Sabbath in the Wilderness and Placed it in the Middle of the Decalogue Because it Was the Sign of the Covenant

Archaeology testifies that the reason God placed the Sabbath in the middle of 9 universal laws was because in ancient, near east treaties, kings often placed the sign of the covenant in the middle of the covenant document.

But, why did the Jews keep the Sabbath in the wilderness (Ex. 16) before the Old Covenant started? Remember when Christ celebrated the Lord's Supper (the sign of the New Covenant) before the New Covenant started, when He shed the blood of the covenant on the Cross? Apparently, covenant parties often celebrated the sign before putting the covenant into effect.

God first "gave" and "revealed" the Sabbath in the Wilderness, not Eden...

> "Mt. Sinai...you *made known* to them your holy Sabbath..." (Neh. 9:14).

> "So I led them out of the land of Egypt and brought them into the wilderness...I *gave* them My Sabbaths..." (Ezek. 20:10, 12).

If they already knew the Sabbath from creation, then how could God make it known in the Wilderness? And, if they already had the Sabbath, then how could He give it to them? Notice in Exodus 16, there's no rebuke to restore the Sabbath. And, He had to explain the instructions on how to keep it because they had never heard.

There's no evidence that Adam, Enoch, Noah, Abraham, Isaac, or Jacob kept the Sabbath. That's because God introduced the 24-hour, weekly Sabbath in the wilderness, not at creation. (By the way, did you know that the Orthodox Jewish rabbis agree that God first gave the Sabbath to Israel in the wilderness, not Adam at creation?)

5. It's Impossible That God Changed the Sabbath Day, Because He Still Calls Saturday *the Sabbath* 13 Times After Christ Rose

It's 100% impossible that God changed the Sabbath from Saturday to Sunday, after Christ rose. We can know this for certain because He still calls Saturday the Sabbath (the day when the Jews met in the synagogue) 5 times in Acts.

"...And on the Sabbath day they went into the synagogue and sat down" (Acts 13:14, cf. 13:27, 15:21, 17:1-2, 18:4, cf. 13:42, 13:44, 16:13).

Plus, God still calls Sunday the "first (day) from the Sabbath" 8 times (Greek: mia Sabbaton, or protos Sabbaton: Mt. 28:1; Mk. 16:2; 16:9; Lk. 24:1; Jn. 20:1, 20:19; Acts 20:7; 1 Cor. 16:2). So, if anyone tries to tell you that God changed the Sabbath from Saturday to Sunday, just tell them, "Mia sabbaton."

Saturday was still THE only Sabbath. Obviously, there could not have been 2 Sabbaths: A Jewish Sabbath on Saturday, followed by a Christian Sabbath on Sunday. In light of these 13 post-resurrection mentions of the Saturday Sabbath, it is impossible that God changed the Sabbath to Sunday.

6. Jewish Authors Criticized the Sabbath Without Exceptions

When I say that the apostles "criticized" the Sabbath and the law, I mean they criticized their misapplication, not as though God made a mistake.

It's unthinkable that a Jewish author like Paul could believe the Sabbath was still binding when he omitted any exceptions in his 3, negative criticisms of the Sabbath (Rom. 14:5-6; Gal. 4:10; Col. 2:16-17). And, surely if the author of Hebrews believed the Sabbath was transferred to Sunday, he would have explained it in Hebrews 4, right?

Have you ever heard a Sabbatarian teach on any of those passages say, "BUT, we know that can't include the Christian Sabbath?" Paul never said "but" because he didn't believe in Sabbatarianism. Just try substituting Sabbatarian exceptions into the verses below, and see how ridiculous they sound...

"Therefore let no one pass judgment on you in questions of food and drink, or with regard to a festival or a new moon or a Sabbath *(except the weekly, Christian Sabbath)*. These are a shadow of the things to come, but the substance belongs to Christ" (Col. 2:16-17).

"One person esteems one day as better than another, while another esteems all days *(except the weekly, Christian Sabbath)* alike. Each one should be fully convinced in his own mind" (Rom. 14:5-6).

"...how can you turn back again to the weak and worthless elementary principles of the world, whose slaves you want to be once more? You observe days *(except the weekly, Christian Sabbath)* and months and seasons and years!" (Gal. 4:9-10).

Can you imagine a Jewish author omitting exceptions like that?

7. We Enter Into God's Eternal Sabbath Rest by Believing the Gospel

"For the gospel came to us...For we who have believed enter that rest" (Heb. 4:2-3).

In Scripture, there are 2 Sabbaths:

1. The big Sabbath: God's eternal rest (Gen. 2; Heb. 4)
2. The little Sabbath: Man's 24-hour, weekly rest (Ex. 16, Ex. 20)

The context of Hebrews 3:11 - 4:11 is God's eternal rest, not man's 24-hour, weekly rest. The words for "rest" appear 12 times, *always* meaning God's eternal rest, *never* man's 24-hour, weekly rest.

But, why does Hebrews 4:9 change the word to "Sabbath-keeping?" Because we are keeping Sabbath by resting in Christ, since we believe the gospel (just like we are circumcised, and keeping Passover in Christ). Notice how the context of v. 9 (before in v. 8 and after in v. 10) speaks of God's eternal rest, not man's 24-hour rest...

"For if Joshua had *given them (eternal) rest,* God would not have spoken of another day later on. *So then,* there remains a *(eternal) Sabbath-keeping* for the people of God, *for* whoever has *entered God's (eternal) rest* has also rested from his works as God did (eternally) from His" (Heb. 4:8-10).

And in Hebrews 4, notice how the 2 other verses with the word "remains" refer to God's eternal Sabbath rest, not man's 24-hour, Sabbath rest...

"Therefore, while the promise of *entering His (eternal) rest still remains...*" (Heb. 4:1).

"They shall not enter My (eternal) rest. Since therefore it *remains* for some to enter (My eternal rest)..." (Heb. 4:5-6).

"So then, there *remains* a (eternal) Sabbath-keeping for the people of God" (Heb. 4:9).

So in Hebrews 4, *all* 12 uses of "rest" refer to God's eternal rest, not man's 24-hour, weekly rest. And, *all* 3 uses of "remains" refer to God's eternal rest, not man's 24-hour, weekly rest. This is the big Sabbath, not the little Sabbath.

This eternal rest of God is the same salvation rest that Jesus invites us to enter: "Come to Me, all those tired of working, and burdened, and *I will give you rest... You will find rest for your souls.*" (Mt. 11:28-29).

What About Decalogue-Evangelism?
The Apostles' Gospel Defined Sin, But Not From the Decalogue

In the 16th - 17th centuries, some of the Reformers and Puritans popularized the idea that we must teach sinners the Ten Commandments in evangelism. And today in the 21st century, many Reformed theologians continue to promote this view. One evangelist who has popularized it is Ray Comfort in his sermon *Hell's Best Kept Secret.*

Comfort's driving motivation is that 80-90% of modern evangelistic "converts" apostatize. And, he diagnoses the problem as a lack of conviction of sin from law-preaching.

Actually, Comfort is right that one of the reasons why "converts" apostatize is because of lack of conviction of sin. He's got the right motivation and diagnosis, but the wrong cure (the wrong law).

Did the apostles evangelize with the Ten Commandments in Acts? Doug Moo challenges Comfort and the traditional Reformed view...

> "Indeed, the popular notion that the Mosaic law should be preached as a preparation for the gospel, revealing sin and one's need of salvation, has slim biblical support. None of the examples of evangelistic preaching in the New Testament uses the law in this way."[7]

This question is easy to answer if you have a Bible that shows Old Testament quotes in the New Testament. Simply look at all the Old Testament quotes in Acts. You'll see Joel 2:28-32; Psalm 110:1, etc., but not Exodus 20:3-17 or Deuteronomy 5:7-21. The apostles never explicitly quoted any of the Ten Commandments in Acts.

Sure, when evangelizing Jews, some of the Ten Commandments were implied, but never explicitly stated or quoted in Acts. For example, when Peter told the Jews at Pentecost that they killed the Messiah, he and his hearers probably thought of the 6th commandment, "You shall not murder."

But, evangelizing the Gentiles is a different story. Look at the apostles' example of evangelizing Gentiles at Mars Hill. (Acts 17:22-31) You won't see any Decalogue explanation there, just conviction of the sin of idolatry. And, since these heathen didn't have the law, Paul's source of authority that idolatry was a sin was the conscience, not the Ten Commandments.

When evangelizing, we can convict sinners by appealing to any of 3 different sources of law:

1. Conscience: "Idolatry is a sin." (No Scripture)

2. The Law of Moses: "You shall not make for yourself a carved image...You shall not bow down to them or serve them..." (Ex. 20:4).

---

[7] Moo in Gundry, 339.

3. The Law of Christ: "But as for...idolaters...their portion will be in the lake that burns with fire..." (Rev. 21:8).

If you're evangelizing Jews, then yes, use the Ten Commandments, and other sins from the law of Moses. But, if you're evangelizing Gentiles, then use the conscience like the apostles did, or the law of Christ by quoting the New Testament. (Even if some evangelists misapply the Ten Commandments to Gentiles, God can still use them to convict of sin.)

Let's take a quick look at the 5 verses most often used to support Decalogue-evangelism: Gal. 3:24; Ps. 19:7; Rom. 3:20, 7:7; and Mt. 19:16-22...

Galatians 3:24
"So then, the law was our guardian *until* Christ came, in order that we might be justified by faith."

Not only does this verse not teach Decalogue-evangelism, it actually teaches the opposite: The temporary function of the Decalogue. As a matter of fact, this is one of the Bible's clearest verses teaching that God cancelled the Decalogue.

First, notice the word "until" in Gal. 3:24 above and Gal. 3:19 below...

"Why then the law? It was added because of transgressions, *until* the offspring (Christ) should come..." (Gal. 3:19).

What both verses are saying is that the law was added from the time of Moses *until* the time of Christ. It regulated the nation of Israel only temporarily.

Second, notice the word "guardian." In the Greek, this word means "guardian" or "tutor" (similar to a nanny). When some rich families have a child, they hire a guardian/tutor/nanny as a live-in babysitter, *until* the child grows up.

So, what Paul is saying is that the law functioned as Israel's guardian until the time of Christ. To claim that we still need to obey the Decalogue today is like claiming that a 30-year old adult still needs a babysitter.

Third, the context of Galatians 3 is about redemption accomplished for the corporate people of God in the 1st century, not redemption applied to individuals from the 1st – 21st centuries. In other words, the law functioned for a one-time, redemptive-historical period, which is not repeatable today.

> Psalms 19:7-11
> "The law of the LORD is perfect, converting the soul…the precepts of the LORD are right, rejoicing the heart…More to be desired are they than gold…sweeter also than honey…by them your servant is warned…" (NKJV).

The first thing we notice is that the ESV and NIV use the word "reviving" instead of "converting." So, is this verse talking about converting unbelievers, or sanctifying believers? Judging by the context, David is rejoicing in the law for his own sanctification.

Plus, Decalogue evangelists interpret the word "law" here as "the Decalogue alone." However, as we saw earlier, the 2 most common meanings for "law" are "all Old Covenant commands" or "the whole Old Testament." David rejoiced in all 613 of God's commands, not merely 10 of them.

> Romans 3:20
> "…through the law comes knowledge of sin."

And, what is the meaning of "law" here? In Rom. 3:9-20, Paul quotes Psalms, Proverbs, and Isaiah, but not Exodus 20. So, "law" here obviously means "the whole Old Testament," not "the Decalogue alone."

> Romans 7:7
> "Yet if it had not been for the law, I would not have known sin. I would not have known what it is to covet if the law had not said, "You shall not covet."

The Holy Spirit convicted Saul, a Jew born under the law, of sin from the command against covetousness. So, if you're evangelizing Jews, feel free to use the Ten Commandments.

Matthew 19:16-22
"…a man came up to him, saying, 'Teacher, what good deed must I do to have eternal life?' And he said to him, 'Why do you ask me about what is good? There is only one who is good. If you would enter life, keep the commandments…You shall not murder, You shall not commit adultery, You shall not steal, You shall not bear false witness, Honor your father and mother, and, You shall love your neighbor as yourself.' The young man said to him, 'All these I have kept. What do I still lack?' Jesus said to him, 'If you would be perfect, go, sell what you possess and give to the poor, and you will have treasure in heaven; and come, follow me.' When the young man heard this he went away sorrowful, for he had great possessions."

Finally, what about the Rich Young Ruler? Here is one example where Christ used some of the Ten Commandments to evangelize a sinner (since the man was likely Jewish), but not to convict him of sin. Remember, the man said that he had obeyed all those commands.

Then, Jesus convicted the man of the sin of loving money by demanding that he sell all his possessions and give to the poor. This was the sin of loving his own possessions, not coveting his neighbors' possessions (the 10th commandment). Jesus used His Lordship, not the Decalogue, to convict the Rich Young Ruler of sin.

In conclusion about Decalogue-evangelism…

1. Jesus evangelized a Jew by quoting from the Decalogue, but not for conviction of sin.

2. The apostles evangelized Jews by implying, but not explicitly quoting, any of the Ten Commandments.

3. The apostles evangelized Gentiles by convicting of sin from the conscience, not the Decalogue.

Also, it's important to remember that true, apostolic evangelism is Christ-centered, not law/sin-centered. The apostles' gospel messages in Acts emphasized Jesus Christ Himself: His Messiahship, miracles, death, resurrection, reign, and return. Conviction of sin was only a means to the end: The person of Christ. That's why it's called "the good news of (about) Jesus Christ."

In summary about the so-called "moral law," the Holy Spirit never says that the Sabbath and the whole Decalogue are the eternal, unchanging, moral law of God. But, He does say that the standard of judgment for all humans, including the Gentiles, is the sin lists.

2. "But Christ Did Not Come to Abolish the Law"

For regulation, or revelation?[8] As Old Covenant contract, or Old Testament Scripture?

Here's a puzzle for you. Which verses are true: Those on the left or right?

Which Verses Are True: Is the Law Abolished or Not Abolished?	
The Law is Not Abolished	**The Law Is Abolished**
"Do not think that I have come to abolish (Gk: kataluo) the Law or the Prophets; I have not come to abolish (Gk. kataluo) them but to fulfill them" (Mt. 5:17-18).	"by abolishing (Gk: katargeo) the law of commandments and ordinances..." (Eph. 2:15).
"Do we then abolish (Gk: katargeo) the law by this faith? By no means! On the contrary, we uphold the law" (Rom. 3:31).	

Of course, they're both true if we believe the Bible is inerrant and inspired by the same sovereign Spirit of God. So, how can we harmonize that the law is abolished, but not abolished?

The Distinction Between the Law for Old Covenant Regulation vs. Old Testament Revelation: How to Harmonize Paul's Negative & Positive Verses on the Law

One reason why this question of the law in the New Testament may be the most complex issue in theology is Paul's seemingly contradictory praise and criticism for the law of Moses. (No, Paul was not a schizophrenic!)

---

[8] Wayne Strickland, "The Inauguration of the Law of Christ With the Gospel," in Gundry, 277-279.

John Owen, the Puritan theologian, had it right when he distinguished 2 important meanings of the word "law."

"The law is taken two ways:

1. For the whole revelation of the mind and will of God in the Old Testament...

2. The covenant rule of perfect obedience: 'Do this, and live.' In this sense men are said to be 'under it, in opposition unto being 'under grace.' They are under its power, rule, conditions, and authority, as a covenant."[9]

Wayne Strickland explains the distinction between regulation vs. revelation...

"...the Mosaic law had a revelatory aspect and regulatory aspect...The revelatory aspect was in mind when Paul discussed the merits of the law...Armed with this understanding of the twofold purpose of the law, the seemingly contradictory assertions of Paul concerning the law may be understood in a harmonious manner."[10]

Another way to explain this distinction is Old Covenant vs. Old Testament. However, that distinction may be confusing since Christians often use those 2 terms synonymously. Yet, if we view those terms historically, the distinction is valid, since the Old Testament starts from Creation, while the Old Covenant starts from Sinai. Old Covenant and Old Testament may be distinguished, but not separated, since Genesis is the introduction to the Old Covenant.

Paul's negative statements about the law often refer to regulation (Old Covenant contract). And, his positive statements often refer to revelation (Old Testament Scripture). This is the solution to harmonize many of Paul's seemingly contradictory statements on the law.

---

[9] John Owen, The Works of John Owen, (Edinburgh: Banner of Truth Trust, 1965), VII: 543.
[10] Wayne Strickland, in Gundry, 277-279.

So, the word "law" has multiple meanings in Scripture. Two of the most important meanings are:

1. Law regulation (Old Covenant contract).
2. Law revelation (Old Testament Scripture).

Those 2 distinctions in the word "law" are clearly demonstrated in these 3 verses...

"...whatever *the law says* (as Old Testament revelation) it speaks to those who are *under the law* (as Old Covenant regulation)..." (Rom. 3:19).

"But, now the righteousness of God has been manifested *apart from the law* (as Old Covenant regulation), although *the Law (Pentateuch) and the Prophets* (as Old Testament revelation) *bear witness* to it." (Rom. 3:21).

"Tell me, you who desire to be *under the law* (as Old Covenant regulation), do you not *listen to the law* (as Old Testament revelation?)" (Gal. 4:21).

There are several other verses demonstrating the Law's revelational function as Old Testament Scripture...

"...What is *written* in the Law? How do you *read* it?" (Lk. 10:26; cf. Mt. 12:5; Lk. 2:23; Jn 8:17, 10:34, 15:25; 2 Cor. 3:14; etc.)

The Law is written, read, heard, and it speaks. That means the law was more than just commands to be obeyed or disobeyed. Do you see the distinction between Old Covenant regulation for obedience vs. Old Testament revelation for doctrine? We use the Old Testament today for doctrine/faith, but not practice.

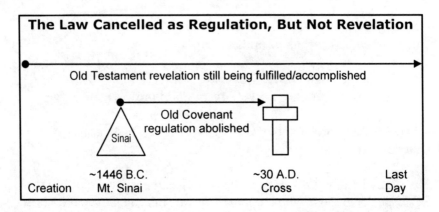

Now, let's apply that distinction between law as regulation vs. revelation to the most crucial passage for understanding our relationship to Old Testament law: The Sermon on the Mount. Here are 2 different interpretations of this key passage...

2 Different Views of, "I Did Not Come to Abolish the Law, But to Fulfill it"	
*Reformed, Covenant Theology	New Covenant Theology
"Do not think that I have come to abolish the Law (the Decalogue alone) or the Prophets.	"Do not think that I have come to abolish the Law (Gen. - Deut.) or the Prophets (Josh.-Mal., the whole O.T.)
I have not come to abolish them but to fulfill (confirm) them (for obedience).	I have not come to abolish them (as O.T. revelation), but to fulfill them (prophetically/ eschatologically cf. Mt. 1:22; 2:15, 17, 23; 4:14; 8:17; 12:17; 13:35; 21:4; 26:54, 56; 27:9; Lk. 24:44; etc.)
For truly, I say to you, until heaven and earth pass away, not an iota, not a dot, will pass from the Law (the Decalogue alone) until all is accomplished.	For truly, I say to you, until heaven and earth pass away, not an iota, not a dot, will pass from the Law (whole Old Testament as revelation) until all is accomplished (prophetically/ eschatologically).
Therefore whoever relaxes one of the least of these commandments (the Decalogue alone) and teaches others to do the same will be called least in the kingdom of heaven..." (Mt. 5:17-19).	Therefore (since I fulfill the law's prophecies) whoever relaxes one of the least of these commandments (of Mine, cf. Mt. 7:24-26; Lk. 6:46-47, 7:1) and teaches others to do the same will be called least in the kingdom of heaven..." (Mt. 5:17-19).

*Covenant theologians have multiple interpretations of this passage. For example, some believe "these commands" refers to Christ's and Moses' commands, since "they must be the same."

Why "Plerosai" Means "Fulfill" Eschatologically, Not "Confirm" for Obedience

In Matthew 5:17, the Greek word "plerosai" is crucial to understanding the whole sermon that Jesus is about to preach. Many earlier Covenant Theologians interpreted "plerosai" as "confirm." They taught that Jesus was confirming/establishing the Decalogue for our obedience.

However, some recent Covenant Theologians have conceded that their forefathers' were wrong because Matthew's normal meaning for "pleroo" refers to eschatological, prophetic, and/or typological fulfillment. (Besides, if Matthew meant "confirm" or "establish" then he should have chosen the Greek words "bebaioo" or "histemi.")

A Parallel Passage to Mt. 5:17-18, Also About Eschatological Fulfillment, Not Confirming the Decalogue for Obedience	
"Do not think I have come to abolish the *Law or the Prophets;* I have not come to abolish them but to *fulfill them.* For truly, I say to you, until heaven and earth pass away, not an iota, not a dot, will pass from the Law until *all is accomplished"* (Mt. 5:17-18).	*"...everything* written about me in the *Law of Moses and the Prophets and the Psalms must be fulfilled"* (Lk. 24:44).

In the 2 passages above, we see 3 parallels:

1. The Law and Prophets
2. All/everything
3. Fulfill/accomplished

So, just as Luke 24:44 refers to fulfilling prophecy instead of confirming the Decalogue for obedience, so does Matthew 5:17-18.

Matthew's normal meaning for "pleroo" is eschatological fulfillment (not obedience) as shown in these 12 examples...

"All this took place to *fulfill* what the Lord had spoken by the prophet" (Mt. 1:22).

"...This was to *fulfill* what the Lord had spoken by the prophet..." (Mt. 2:15).

"Then was *fulfilled* what was spoken by the prophet Jeremiah" (Mt. 2:17).

"...that what was spoken by the prophets might be *fulfilled*..." (Mt. 2:23).

"so that what was spoken by the prophet Isaiah might be *fulfilled*" (Mt. 4:14).

"This was to *fulfill* what was spoken by the prophet Isaiah..." (Mt. 8:17).

"This was to *fulfill* what was spoken by the prophet Isaiah" (Mt. 12:17).

"This was to *fulfill* what was spoken by the prophet" (Mt. 13:35).

"This took place to *fulfill* what was spoken by the prophet, saying" (Mt. 21:4).

"But how then should the Scriptures be *fulfilled* that it must be so?" (Mt. 26:54).

"But all this has taken place that the Scriptures of the prophets might be *fulfilled*" (Mt. 26:56).

"Then was *fulfilled* what had been spoken by the prophet Jeremiah, saying" (Mt. 27:9).

Notice that all those uses of "pleroo" refer to revelation (Old Testament), not regulation (Old Covenant). And, it's the same in the Sermon on the Mount. Jesus came to fulfill the Old Testament prophecies and types as revelation, not to confirm the Old Covenant Decalogue alone for regulation.

In the first century, the goal of redemptive history finally started arriving when Messiah fulfilled prophecy as the better Prophet, better Priest, and better King. As the new Prophet, He gave new prophecies and teachings. As the new Priest, He made a new sacrifice. And, as the new King, He gave a new law.

"Law or Prophets" Means the "Whole Old Testament" (Not the "Ten Commandments Alone")

Yes, Christ did not come to destroy the law or prophets. And, what is the meaning of the phrase "law or prophets" (cf. "law and prophets")?

It never once means "Ten Commandments and prophets." It always means the "Pentateuch and prophets," a.k.a. "Genesis - Deuteronomy and the Prophets," a.k.a. the "whole Old Testament."

John MacArthur agrees that "Law or Prophets" refers to the whole Old Testament and its continuing revelation…

> *"The phrase 'the Law and the Prophets' speaks of the entirety of the OT Scriptures…* Here Christ emphasizes both the inspiration and the enduring authority of all Scripture. He specifically affirms the utter inerrancy and absolute authority of the OT as the Word of God - down to the least jot and tittle. Again (see note on v. 17), we should not think that the NT supplants or completely abrogates the OT but instead fulfills and explicates it. For example, all the ceremonial requirements of the Mosaic Law are fulfilled in Christ and are no longer to be observed by Christians (Col. 2:16, 17). Yet not one jot or tittle is thereby erased; the underlying truths of those Scriptures remain…"[11]

And, Don Carson agrees that Christ is speaking of not destroying the Old Testament…

---

[11] John MacArthur, *The MacArthur Bible Commentary*, (Nashville: Nelson, 2005), 1130.

"In no case does this 'abolish' the Old Testament as canon, any more than the obsolescence of the Levitical sacrificial system abolishes tabernacle ritual as canon."[12]

So, Christ did not come to destroy "Genesis - Deuteronomy or the Prophets." In other words, He did not come to destroy the law as Old Testament revelation. (The error that the Old Testament was abolished as Scripture was popularized later in church history by the heretic Marcion.)

6 Reasons Why "These Commandments" Refers to "Christ's Commands," Instead of "Moses' Commands"

In Matthew 5:19, does the phrase "these commandments" refer to Moses' commands or Christ's commands? (Although, some Covenant Theologians think that Moses' commands = Christ's commands.)

1. Since "Law or Prophets" Means "the Whole Old Testament," Then if "These Commandments" Means "Moses' Laws" it Must Include All of Moses' Laws

Since "Law or Prophets" means "the whole Old Testament," Covenant Theology is trapped in a dilemma...

> 1. Christ did not come to abolish the Law or Prophets (whole O.T.)
> 2. We can't relax one of Moses' commands (from the whole O.T.)
> 3. Therefore, we must obey all of Moses' commands (from the whole O.T.)

Do you see Covenant Theology's problem? Since "Law or Prophets" clearly means the "whole Old Testament," if "these commands" means "Moses commands," then we must obey every jot and tittle of all Old Testament commands, including the Ten Commandments, and so-called "civil and ceremonial laws."

---

[12] Don Carson, "Matthew," in *The Expositor's Bible Commentary*, Frank E. Gaebelein, Ed., (Grand Rapids: Zondervan, 1984), 8:143-144.

But, if "these commands" means Christ's commands, then the dilemma is solved. "Christ's commands" is far less problematic.

2. Both the Sermon on the Mount and its Parallel Sermon on the Plain Emphasize Obeying Christ's Words

In the Sermon on the Mount (Mt. 5:1 – 7:29) and the Sermon on the Plain (Lk. 6:20 - 7:1) Christ tells us to do (obey) His words...

> "Everyone then who hears *these words of Mine and does them*... And everyone who hears *these words of Mine and does not do them...* " (Mt. 7:24, 26. The conclusion to the Sermon on the Mount).

> "Everyone who comes to Me and hears *My words and does them*... But the one who hears and does not do them..." (Lk. 6:47, 49).

> "After he had finished all *His sayings* in the hearing of the people..." (Lk. 7:1).

> "teaching them to observe all that *I have commanded* you..." (cf. Mt. 28:20, by the same author).

In these verses above, there is much evidence that Christ is speaking of His commands.

3. The Sermon on the Mount Includes at Least 7 Commands Not in the Decalogue

Another reason that Christ could not have been referring to Moses' commands is that the Sermon on the Mount includes several topics not even in the Decalogue, such as:

> 1. Retaliation
> 2. Love your enemies
> 3. Giving
> 4. Prayer
> 5. Money
> 6. Worry
> 7. Judging

So, those topics were all Jesus' commands, not Moses' commands.

4. Since the Parallel Passage (Lk. 16:17) Says the Kingdom of God Is After John, Therefore the Commandments of the Kingdom Are After John

The Law and Prophets Were Until ~30 A.D., Then the Kingdom of God Is After ~30 A.D.	
"The Law and the Prophets were *until* John; *since then* the good news of the *kingdom of God* is preached, and everyone forces his way into it. But it is easier for *heaven and earth to pass away than for one dot of the Law (O.T. prophesy) to become void"* (Lk. 16:17).	"Do not think that I have come to abolish *the Law or the Prophets;* I have not come to abolish them but to fulfill them For truly, I say to you, *until heaven and earth pass away, not an iota, not a dot, will pass from the Law* (O.T. prophecy) until all is accomplished. Therefore whoever relaxes one of the least of *these commandments* and teaches others to do the same will be called least in the kingdom of heaven, but whoever does them and teaches them will be called great in the *kingdom of heaven* (Mt. 5:17-19).

These 2 parallel passages share 5 ideas:

1. The Law and/or Prophets
2. Not a dot/iota of the Law
3. Will become void/pass away
4. Heaven and earth pass away
5. The Kingdom of God/heaven

In Luke 16:17, notice how "the Law and Prophets" refers to the time before Christ, while "the kingdom of God" refers to the time after Christ. So in Matthew 5:19, "these commands…in the kingdom of heaven" refers to the time of the kingdom of heaven after Christ, not the Law and Prophets before Christ.

5. The Typology Between the Giving of the Old Law at Sinai vs.
the New Law at the Sermon on the Mount

There's another reason why Jesus is likely giving a new law in the
Sermon on the Mount. He was the antitype fulfillment of Moses
and Israel. Many scholars agree that Matthew portrays several
parallel events between Moses/Israel and Christ. (Although, like
most types - antitypes, those parallels are only partial, not 100%.)
Here are 6 of those parallel events from old to new...

6 Typological Events by Moses/Israel and Jesus	
Moses & Israel (the Types)	**Jesus (the Antitype)**
Old Baby Hidden From Genocide "Then Pharaoh commanded all his people, 'Every son that is born to the Hebrews you shall cast into the Nile'...she hid him three months" (Ex. 1:22 – 2:2).	**New Baby Hidden From Genocide** "Rise, take the child and his mother, and flee to Egypt, and remain there until I tell you, for Herod is about to search for the child, to destroy him" (Mt. 2:13).
Old Return After Persecutor's Death "Go back to Egypt, for al the men who were seeking your life are dead" (Ex. 4:19).	**New Return After Persecutor's Death** "...Rise, take the child and his mother and go to the land of Israel, for those who sought the child's life are dead" (Mt. 2:15-20).
Old Exodus "When Israel was a child, I loved him, and out of Egypt I called my son" (Hos. 11:1). "...all the host of the LORD went out from the land of Egypt" (Ex. 12:41).	**New Exodus** "This was to fulfill what the Lord had spoken by the prophet, 'Out of Egypt I called my son.'" (Mt. 2:15)

Old Baptism	New Baptism
"And the LORD went before them by day in a pillar of cloud...And the people of Israel went into the midst of the sea on dry ground, the waters being a wall to them on their right hand and on their left" (Ex. 13:21, 14:22). "...our fathers were all under the cloud, and all passed through the sea, and all were baptized into Moses in the cloud and in the sea..." (1 Cor. 10:1-2).	"...Jesus was baptized..." (Mt. 3:16).
Old Temptations in the Wilderness	**New Temptations in the Wilderness**
"Then Moses made Israel set out from the Red Sea, and they went into the wilderness...There the LORD...tested them..." (Ex. 15:22, 25). "And the whole congregation of the people of Israel grumbled against Moses and Aaron in the wilderness..." (Ex. 16:2). "And he humbled you and let you hunger and fed you with manna...that he might make you know that man does not live by bread alone, but man lives by every word that comes from the mouth of the LORD" (Deut. 8:3).	"Then Jesus was led up by the Spirit into the wilderness to be tempted by the devil. And after fasting forty days and forty nights, he was hungry" (Mt. 3:1-2). "Man shall not live by bread alone, but by every word that comes from the mouth of God" (Mt. 4:4).

"...And Moses said to them, 'Why do you quarrel with me? Why do you test the LORD?' But the people thirsted there for water, and the people grumbled against Moses..." (Ex. 17:2-3). "You shall not put the LORD your God to the test, as you tested him at Massah" (Deut. 6:16).	"You shall not put the Lord your God to the test" (Mt. 4:7).
"It is the LORD your God you shall fear. Him you shall serve..." (Deut. 6:13). "You shall fear the LORD your God. You shall serve him..." (Deut. 10:20).	You shall worship the Lord your God and him only shall you serve" (Mt. 4:10).
Old Law Given From a Mountain	**New Law Given From a Mountain**
"And the LORD called Moses to the top of the mountain, and Moses went up...And God spoke all these words saying..." (Ex. 19:20 - 20:1ff.)	"Seeing the crowds, he went up on the mountain...these commandments...these words..." (Mt. 5:1, 19, 7:24, 7:26).

Notice in all 6 events above, Jesus did not repeat the exact, same events as Moses and Israel. He accomplished similar, but new events.

Jesus wasn't baptized with Israel's same, old baptism in the cloud and sea, but with a new baptism in the river. Also, He didn't face Israel's same, old temptations, but new ones. And, He didn't restate Israel's same, old law from Mt. Sinai, but gave a new law from a new mountain.

6. "These Words" (Ex. 20:1) and "These Commandments" (Mt. 5:19) Are Parallel, and Look Forward, Not Backward

In the chart above, the last parallel is that Moses wrote, "And God spoke all *these words...* " (Ex. 20:1ff.) looking forward to giving His law, not backward. And, Jesus spoke about *"these commandments"* (Mt. 5:19ff.) looking forward to giving His law, not backward to Moses commands in "the Law and the Prophets."

So, there are 6 reasons why "these commandments" more likely refers to "Christ's commandments," than "Moses' commandments." And, in the Sermon on the Mount, Jesus spoke about not abolishing the whole law as Old Testament Scripture, but fulfilling it prophetically.

3. "But the Law Is Written on the Heart in the New Covenant"

Which law: The Old Covenant, law of Moses, or the New Covenant, law of Christ?

God revealed His law progressively in redemptive history. The law of God changed from the law of Moses to the law of Christ. Here is the passage in question...

> "...I will make a New Covenant with the house of Israel and the house of Judah, not like the covenant (a.k.a. Decalogue) that I made with their fathers on the day that I took them by the hand to bring them out of the land of Egypt, my covenant that they broke...*I will put my law within them, and I will write it on their hearts.* And I will be their God, and they shall be My people And no longer shall each one teach his neighbor and each his brother, saying, 'Know the LORD, for they shall all know me, from the least of them to the greatest, declares the LORD. For I will forgive their iniquity, and I will remember their sin no more" (Jer. 31:31-34; cf. Heb. 8:8-12).

What does it mean that God "writes" His law on our hearts? Obviously, He didn't engrave visible printing in 12-point, black, Times Roman font. When we compare Jeremiah 31:31-34 with Hebrews 8:8-12, the contexts contrast 2 peoples: Those who were mostly unregenerate and disobedient vs. those who are all regenerate and obedient.

7 Contrasts Between the Old Covenant vs. the New Covenant in Jer. 31:31-34 "I will make a New Covenant… *NOT* like the covenant that I made with their fathers"		
	Old Covenant Israel: Mostly Unregenerate & Disobedient	**New Covenant Church: All Regenerate & Obedient**
1. Perseverance	"My covenant that they broke"	(My covenant that they will not break.)
2. Obedience	(I will not put my law within them, and I will not write it on their hearts.)	"I will put my law within them, and I will write it on their hearts"
3. God's Faithfulness	(I will not be their God.)	"I will be their God"
4. Israel's Faithfulness	(They shall not be my people.)	"They shall be my people"
5. Evangelism	(They shall each one teach his neighbor and each his brother, saying, "Know the LORD.")	"No longer shall each one teach his neighbor and each his brother, saying, 'Know the LORD'"
6. Salvation	(They shall not all know me.)	"They shall all know me"
7. Forgiveness	(I will not forgive their iniquity, and I will remember their.)	"I will forgive their iniquity, and I will remember their sin no more."

Notice that all 7 New Covenant blessings above imply regeneration and obedience (blessings which most of Old Covenant Israel lacked). So, "I will write My laws on their hearts" is likely a metaphor for "I will regenerate their hearts to obey My laws."

By the way, Old Testament saints (the regenerate remnant) probably already had all 7 of those blessings, including the law of Moses written on their hearts and in the Old Testament. (So, New Covenant saints have the law of Christ written on their hearts and in the New Testament.)

The main difference between the Old vs. the New in Jeremiah 31 is the salvation of a few vs. all: Few in Old Covenant Israel were saved, all in the New Covenant Church are saved.

And, that's why we baptize only believers, instead of believers and their infants. The Old Covenant was a family covenant that included unregenerate adults and their infants. But, the New Covenant is an individual's covenant that includes only the regenerate.

Now, let's compare Jer. 31:33-34 with 2 parallel passages…

3 Parallel Passages on Regeneration And Obedience to God's Commands		
Jer. 31:33-34	**Ezek. 11:19-20**	**Ezek. 36:26-27**
"I will put *my law* within them, and I will write it on their hearts. And I will be their God, and they shall be my people. And no longer shall each one teach his neighbor and each his brother, saying, 'Know the LORD,' for they shall all know me…I will forgive their iniquity, and I will remember their sin no more."	"And I will give them one heart, and *a new spirit* I will put within them. I will remove the heart of stone from their flesh and give them a *heart of flesh,* that they may *walk in my statutes and keep my rules and obey them.* And they shall be my people, and I will be their God."	"And I will give you *a new heart, and a new spirit* I will put within you. And I will remove the heart of stone from your flesh and give you a heart of flesh. And I will put my spirit within you, and cause you to *walk in my statures and be careful to obey my rules."*

In these 3 passages, we see 3 common themes:

1. Regeneration: a heart of flesh/new heart (implied in Jer. 31).
2. Spirit's indwelling: a new spirit/my Spirit (implied in Jer. 31).
3. Obedience to rules: my law/obey my statutes and my rules.

Our sovereign God guarantees that all His New Covenant people will have new hearts, and the indwelling Spirit to obey Him. But, which laws does He "write on the heart" (for us to obey?)

In *Defense of the Decalogue*, Richard Barcellos claims that...

> "Exodus 24:12 identifies the 'tablets of stone' with 'the law and commandments which I have written.' This is a very important verse, for it uses the Hebrew word torah [law] as a synonym for what God wrote on stones."[13]

OK, all that proves is that there is only one verse in the whole Bible where the word "law" probably means "the Decalogue alone." But, there are hundreds of verses where "law" means:

1. All Old Covenant commands.
2. The Pentateuch or the whole Old Testament.

One of Covenant Theology's common errors is to assume that the phrase "the law" when used positively must mean "the Decalogue *alone*," but when used negatively it must mean "the whole law except the Decalogue." They fail to see that "law" used positively often means the "whole Pentateuch" or "whole Old Testament."

> **"One of Covenant Theology's common errors is to assume that the phrase "the law" when used positively means "the Decalogue ALONE," but when used negatively means "the whole law EXCEPT the Decalogue."**

---

[13] Richard C. Barcellos, *Defense of the Decalogue*, (Enumclaw, WA: Winepress Publishing, 2001), 18

Barcellos also argues that the law referred to in Jeremiah 31:33 must have already been in existence at the time of Jeremiah, and it must be the Decalogue. However, here are 6 problems with that interpretation...

1. Jeremiah uses the word "law" 12 times. But, never once does it mean "the Decalogue alone."

2. Since the house of Israel and the house of Judah were already in existence then, must they also be the same today? In other words, is this prophecy fulfilled only by Jews, not the Church (with Jews and Gentiles?)

In Ezekiel 40-48, will Covenant Theologians argue consistently that since the temple, priests, and sacrifices were already in existence then, they must be the same today?

In some Old Testament prophecies and Hebrews, why does Covenant Theology often use New Testament definitions of "priest, sacrifices, temple, and Israel," but an Old Testament definition of "law?"

> **"In the Prophets and Hebrews, why does Covenant Theology often use New Testament definitions of 'priest, sacrifices, temple, and Israel,' but an Old Testament definition of 'law?'"**

Covenant Theology applies their O.T. - N.T., prophetic hermeneutic inconsistently and selectively.

3. After being regenerated, no Gentile heathen convert has ever testified to knowing his duty to keep the Sabbath. The Sabbath has to be taught to converts, because the Holy Spirit doesn't teach it at regeneration. So, God doesn't write the whole Decalogue on regenerate hearts.

4. It's an oxymoron to claim that a new covenant contains the same old law. Since every covenant (treaty) contains laws, then a new covenant must contain new laws. It is a new contract.

5. Are the Ten Commandments the only laws God "writes on our hearts" to obey? Seems reductionistic, doesn't it? Or, does He write on our hearts all His laws? Doesn't He also motivate us to obey these laws:

- Love the Lord with all your heart?
- Love your neighbor as yourself?
- Love one another as I have loved you?
- Husbands love your wife?
- Deny yourself and take up your cross?

And, what about the new commands which didn't exist at the time of Jeremiah?

- Baptism?
- The Lord's Supper?
- Choose elders and deacons?
- Marry believers only?
- Evangelize the Gentiles?

Does He write on our hearts only the Decalogue, but not also the command for husbands to love their wives? I believe He motivates us to obey all of His commands, not merely 10 of them.

6. When Jeremiah wrote, the word "law" meant the "whole law," not "part of the law." It meant "all Old Covenant commands," not "the Decalogue alone." In other words, it included the so-called "moral, ceremonial, and civil laws." That's exactly how the Jews in Jeremiah's time would have understood it.

So, if you interpret Jeremiah 31:33 literally, then in the New Covenant, God must write all the so-called "moral, civil, and ceremonial" commands on our hearts. (As we'll see later, the 3-part division of the law wasn't even invented until the 13th century, 1800 years after Jeremiah!)

The real issue is, "What are the main hermeneutics for interpreting Old Testament prophecy fulfilled in the New Testament?" May I suggest that these hermeneutics are known by 4 related names...

- The progressive revelation hermeneutic
- The apostles' hermeneutic
- The New Testament hermeneutic
- The New Covenant hermeneutic

All Christians use the New Covenant hermeneutic sometimes. Unfortunately, they rarely apply it consistently.

Sometimes, Covenant Theologians use a "regressive hermeneutic." This results in regressive revelation, instead of progressive revelation (God revealing His redemptive plan gradually and progressively throughout redemptive history).

Regressive Revelation vs. Progressive Revelation	
Reformed, Covenant Theology's Regressive Hermeneutic on Law	**New Covenant Theology's Progressive Hermeneutic on Law**
"The Old Testament is in the New Testament concealed. The New Testament is in the Old Testament revealed."	"The New Testament is in the Old Testament concealed. The Old Testament is in the New Testament revealed."

Progressive revelation allows the New Testament to interpret the Old Testament, not vice-versa. The old saying is true: "The New Testament is in the Old Testament concealed. And, the Old Testament is in the New Testament revealed."

When there is an apparent contradiction between the teaching of the Old Testament and New Testament, the New always takes priority. We need to learn to apply a consistent, New Testament hermeneutic to the Old Testament, including the issues of prophecy, law, church, and kingdom.

Inconsistent, Old-New Covenant Hermeneutics Vs. a Consistent, New Covenant Hermeneutic			
	Roman Catholicism (Inconsistent)	Reformed, Covenant Theology (Inconsistent)	New Covenant Theology (Consistent)
Priest	Old + New (Humans + Christ)	New (Christ)	New (Christ)
Sacrifices	Old + New (The cross + the mass)	New (The cross)	New (The cross)
Theocracy	Old (state-Church)	Theonomists: Old Non-theonomists: New	New (No state-Church)
People Of God	Old (Members & their children)	Paedobaptists: Old + New (Believers & their children) Baptists: New (believers alone)	New (Believers)
Law	2.5/3 Old + New (Moral + civil + part ceremonial + N.T.)	1/3-2/3 Old + New (Moral [+ civil?] + N.T.)	New (N.T.)

For example, when the Old Testament teaches multiple, human priests, but the New Testament later teaches one, Divine-human priest, the New takes priority over the Old. And, when the Old Testament teaches multiple sacrifices for sin, but the New Testament later teaches one sacrifice for sin, the New changes the Old.

Likewise, when the Old Testament teaches the law given by Moses, but the New Testament teaches the law given by Christ (and His apostles) the New changes the Old. The law of God was changed from the law of Moses to the law of Christ.

> **"The law of God was changed from the law of Moses to the law of Christ."**

"for when there is a change in the priesthood, *there is necessarily a change in the law* as well" (Heb. 7:12).

Yes, in the New Covenant God "writes on our hearts" (regenerates us to obey) His law. But, that law is His New Covenant law given by Christ and His apostles, not the whole Decalogue alone given through Moses.

Remember when Peter saw Christ transfigured, next to Moses and Elijah (representing the Law and Prophets?) Peter offered to make 3 tents for them, as though they were equal. But, God spoke from heaven, "This is my beloved Son, with Whom I am well pleased; listen to Him." Listen to the final authority of the Son, Who is the new Prophet and the new Lawgiver.

4. "But There Is One Covenant of Grace"

Do you mean there's one covenant of grace, or one purpose of grace?

The *Westminster Confession of Faith* claims...

"There are not therefore two covenants of grace, differing in substance, but one and the same, under various dispensations."[14]

How many plan(s) and covenant(s) does God have? Here are the 3 popular, answers...

How Many Plan(s) & Covenant(s) Does God Have? 3 Popular Views			
	Reformed, Covenant Theology	**New Covenant Theology**	**Historic Dispensationalism**
# of Plan(s)	One plan of grace: Incl. both Jews & Gentiles	One plan of grace: Incl. both Jews & Gentiles	Two plans: One for Israel, one for the Church
# of Covenant(s)	One covenant of grace	2 major covenants: The Old & the New	Multiple covenants

Covenant Theology teaches that in eternity past, God made a Covenant of Redemption with His Son to redeem the elect. But, the Holy Spirit's inspired terminology for God's pre-historical program is "purpose," "plan," or "will," not "Covenant of Redemption." In the Bible, all Covenants were executed in history, not in pre-historical, eternity past.

---

[14] *The Westminster Confession of Faith*, VII:VI.

Covenant Theology also teaches that in redemptive history, God made a Covenant of Grace with Adam (Gen. 3:15). This one Covenant of Grace, He administered first through Moses, then through Christ. However, this makes the New Covenant merely a new administration of the Old Covenant.

Historic Dispensationalism taught that God had 2 purposes, one for Israel, and one for the Church. (Most Dispensationalists today no longer believe that.) And, they taught multiple covenants.

One Purpose (Singular), Not Two Purposes (Plural)

So, how many plan(s) does God have: One or two? The Holy Spirit uses only the singular plan/purpose, never the plural plans/purposes. So on this point, historic Dispensationalism is wrong, and Covenant Theology is right...

"And we know that for those who love God all things work together for good, for those who are called according to *His purpose"* (Rom. 8:28).

"making known to us the mystery of *His will,* according to *His purpose,* which He set forth in Christ as a *plan... "* (Eph. 1:9-10)

"...having been predestined according to *the purpose* of Him who works all things according to the counsel of *His will"* (Eph. 1:11).

"according to *the eternal purpose* which He has realized in Christ Jesus our Lord" (Eph. 3:11).

"who has saved us and called us to a holy calling, not because of our works, but because of *His own purpose* and grace, which He gave us in Christ Jesus before the ages began" (2 Tim. 1:9).

Multiple Covenants (Plural), Not One Covenant (Singular)

And, how many covenant(s) does God have: One or more? The Holy Spirit uses the plural "covenants." So on this point, historic Dispensationalism is right, and Covenant Theology is wrong...

"They are Israelites, and to them belong...*the covenant*S, the giving of the law..." (Rom. 9:4).

"Who has made us competent to be ministers of *the New Covenant...*" (2 Cor. 3:6).

"...these women are *the two covenant*S..." (Gal. 4:24).

"...strangers to *the covenant*S of promise..." (Eph. 2:12).

"For if *that first covenant* had been faultless...*a second*" (Heb. 8:7.

"I will establish *a New Covenant* with the house of Israel and with the house of Judah, *not like the covenant that I made with their fathers...*" (Heb. 8:8-9).

"In speaking of *a New Covenant,* He has made *the first one* obsolete..." (Heb. 8:13).

"...Jesus, the mediator of *a New Covenant...*" (Heb. 12:24).

So, God has one eternal plan/purpose (of grace) revealed in history by multiple covenants. And, that pre-historical, eternal purpose in Christ organizes all the covenants in history.

One reason why Covenant Theologians can't understand this is because they assume the Old Covenant must be a covenant of salvation from sin. However, Old Covenant saints were saved by God's grace, through faith, during the Old Covenant, but not by the Old Covenant. The Old Covenant was revealed by God's grace, but based on works.

"Old Covenant saints were saved by God's grace, through faith, during the Old Covenant, but not by the Old Covenant."

Obviously, the Old Covenant didn't save all who were in it, since most perished under God's wrath. It didn't effectually save anyone any more than did the covenant with Noah. But, the New Covenant saves all who are in it, thus making it a covenant of salvation.

4 Reasons Why the Old Covenant Was
A Covenant Based on Works, Not "the Covenant of Grace"

God never intended to promise Israel eternal life by obeying Moses' Covenant. They already had the gospel revealed in the promise of Abraham's seed (Gal. 3:8). God gave them the law for "sanctification," not justification. (Although, their "sanctification" blessings were merely physical types, not the spiritual realities, since most of them were unregenerate.)

This can be seen in the typology between Israel and the Church...

Typology Between Israel and the Church	
Israel	**Church**
1. Physical slavery to Egypt.	1. Spiritual slavery to sin.
2. Physical redemption from Egypt.	2. Spiritual redemption from sin.
3. Giving of the law at Sinai	3. Giving of the law at Sermon on the Mt.

Just as God gave the law of Christ to a spiritually redeemed people, so He gave the law of Moses to a physically redeemed people. He gave both the law of Moses to Israel and the law of Christ to the Church for "sanctification," not justification.

1. Kingdom of Priests by Works: If the Israelites obeyed, then they would become (in the future) a kingdom of priests and a holy nation. But, the New Covenant Church already is a kingdom of priests and a holy nation...

Old Covenant Blessing Based on Works	New Covenant Blessing Based on Grace
"...*if* you will indeed obey My voice and keep My covenant, *then...you shall be (in the future)* to Me a kingdom of priests and a holy nation" (Ex. 19:5-6).	"But you *are (presently)* a chosen race, a royal priesthood, a holy nation, a people for His own possession..." (1 Pet. 2:9).

2. No Effectual, Saving Grace: The Old Covenant did not give effectual grace. If you believe the Old Covenant was based on grace, was that grace effectual, or ineffectual? The fact that some were fully in the Old Covenant, but not regenerate means that it could not have been a covenant of effectual grace. However, all New Covenant members have received effectual, saving grace.

If there was ever only one, stiff-necked, unbelieving, rebellious Israelite in the Old Covenant, then it could not have been a covenant of salvation by grace. In other words, it's impossible to be in a covenant of saving grace, yet be unsaved.

3. Apostasy: Israel could break the covenant and apostatize by works, without being preserved by God...

"...The house of Israel and the house of Judah have *broken my covenant* that I made with their fathers" (Jer. 11:10).

"She saw that for all the adulteries of that faithless one, Israel, I had sent her away with a decree of *divorce...*" (Jer. 3:8).

"...You have *broken my covenant,* in addition to all your abominations" (Ezek. 44:7).

Granted, both the Old and New Covenants contain warnings against apostasy. However, the grace for perseverance is guaranteed in the New Covenant, but not the Old Covenant. The Lord guarantees we will persevere because of His regeneration, His Spirit, His promises, His sovereignty, and His faithfulness.

Israel apostatized from the Old Covenant because of their works. But, the New Covenant Church can not and will not ever apostatize.

4. Not of Faith: The Old Covenant was based on human works, not grace, faith, and God's righteousness. (Although, God was motivated by grace to reveal the Old Covenant, its terms were based on works)...

> "But now the righteousness of God has been manifested *apart from the law...*" (Rom. 3:21).

> "For Moses writes about *the righteousness that is based on the law,* that the person who does the commandments shall live by them. *But the righteousness based on faith...*" (Rom. 10:5-6).

> "*...for if justification were through the law,* then Christ died for no purpose" (Gal. 2:21).

> "*But the law is not of faith,* rather 'the one who does them shall live by them'" (Gal. 3:12; cf. Lev. 18:5).

> "*...if a law had been given that could give life, then righteousness would indeed be by the law*" (Gal. 3:21).

Many theologians who agree that the law is based on works, not faith, also acknowledge that the law offered life (Mt. 19:17; Rom. 10:5). They resolve this tension by claiming that the offer of life was merely "hypothetical." In other words, if any Jew could have obeyed perfectly, then he would have been justified. But, no one ever did, nor ever will.

Another possible solution is that for sanctification by works, the law offered final life (glorification), not initial life (justification). Remember, God had already "redeemed" Israel, and placed them in a relationship with Him.

Once you understand that God gave His effectual saving grace, during the Old Covenant, but not by the Old Covenant, all the above problems melt away. The Old Covenant symbolized the gospel found outside that covenant. In the Old Covenant, the gospel was merely typified and symbolized, but not promised.

Just as Noah's covenant didn't save anyone, so the Old Covenant didn't save anyone. Old Testament saints were saved through the gospel promises about Messiah.

Galatians 3:15-25, explains how redemptive history progressed from...

1. Promise (Abraham)
2. Law (Moses)
3. Fulfillment (Christ)[15]

So, the unity of God's purpose (and the unity of the Scriptures) are true. But, there is diversity in God's 2 major covenants.

If you still have questions about one covenant of grace vs. one plan of grace/multiple covenants, see the insightful article *Is There a Covenant of Grace?* by Jon Zens at SearchingTogether.org.

---

[15] Author?, "Gal. 3: Promise/Law/Faith" in *Baptist Reformation Review*, Jon Zens, Ed., Winter 1981, pp.?.

5. "But We Do Not Void the Law, We Uphold it"

"Do we then void the law by this faith? By no means! On the contrary, we uphold the law" (Rom. 3:31).

Uphold it for what: Obedience, or teaching justification by faith? For regulation, or revelation?

2 Different Views of "We Do Not Void the Law, But Uphold It"	
Reformed, Covenant Theology	**New Covenant Theology**
"Do we then void (part of) the law (the Decalogue alone) by this faith? By no means! On the contrary, we uphold (part of) the law (the Decalogue alone for obedience)" (Rom. 3:31).	"Do we then void the law (the whole Old Testament as revelation) by this faith? By no means! On the contrary, we uphold the law (the whole Old Testament for teaching justification by faith)" (Rom. 3:31).

Notice that the context of Romans 3:31 both before (3:26-30) and after (4:1-6ff.) is justification by faith, not works. So, we uphold the law as Old Testament revelation because it teaches justification by faith, apart from works. The context says nothing about the Ten Commandments, or obedience to the law.

Therefore, what Paul is saying in Romans 3:31 is, "Justification by faith apart from Old Covenant law-works does not contradict the Old Testament as law revelation, since it also teaches the same view. Your Old Testament law says that God justified Abraham and David by faith, not works. Therefore, we uphold the Old Testament, instead of voiding it."

6. "But the Law Is Holy, Righteous, and Good"

"What then shall we say? That the law is sin? By no means!
Yet if it had not been for the law, I would not have known sin.
I would not have known what it is to covet if the law had not
said, 'You shall not covet.'...So the law is holy, and the
commandment is holy, and righteous, and good" (Rom. 7:7,
12, cf. 3:19a, 3:20b).

Good for what: Gentile converts' sanctification, or Jewish
evangelism?

Clearly, Paul's reason why the law is good is because it convicted
him of sin when he was still living in the flesh. So, yes the law is
inherently good, not evil, for evangelizing Jews.

7. "But All Scripture Is God-Breathed and Useful"

How Is All Old Testament Scripture Useful: For Faith and Obedience, or Only Faith?	
Faith and Obedience (Reformed, Covenant Theology)	**Faith (New Covenant Theology)**
"All Scripture (the whole O.T.) is breathed out by God and profitable for teaching, for reproof, for correction, and for training in righteousness (including obedience to part of Scripture, the Decalogue only), that the man of God may be competent, equipped for every good work" (2 Tim. 3:16-17).	"All Scripture (the whole O.T.) is breathed out by God and profitable for teaching, for reproof, for correction, and for training in righteousness (faith, but not obedience), that the man of God may be competent, equipped for every good work" (2 Tim. 3:16-17).

This is another one of those arguments for Covenant Theology that does more harm than good. Here's their dilemma...

1. "All Scripture" at that time primarily meant the whole Old Testament.

2. If "teaching, reproof, correction, and training in righteousness" includes obedience...

3. Then we must obey the whole Old Testament (including the so-called "moral, ceremonial, and civil laws.")

Can you see the dilemma? They try to interpret "all Scripture" first as "the whole Old Testament" then second as "some Old Testament laws." So, they make "all Scripture" = "part of Scripture."

A much more feasible interpretation is that "teaching, rebuke, correction, and training in righteousness" does not include obedience to Old Testament laws. In other words, the whole Old Testament is useful for doctrine and faith, but not practice. It trains us in righteousness by doctrine, encouragement, example, warning, etc.

Meredith Kline, former Westminster Seminary professor (who taught that the Old Testament is not the canon governing the Church), observed,

> "...the character of all Scripture as equally the word of God...for the Old Testament Scripture the place it has actually held in the faithful church from the beginning. It is able to make wise unto salvation through faith in Jesus Christ. It is profitable for doctrine, reproof, correction, and instruction in righteousness. As Scriptural revelation the Old Testament provides norms for faith."[16]

Can Covenant Theology use the so-called "ceremonial and civil laws" for teaching, reproof, correction, and training in righteousness? Then, New Covenant Theology can also use the Decalogue for the same 4 purposes.

> **"Can Covenant Theology use the so-called 'ceremonial and civil laws' for teaching, reproof, correction, and training in righteousness? Then, NCT can also use the Decalogue for the same 4 purposes."**

---

[16] Kline, 101.

8. "But Old Testament Commands Are Quoted in the New Testament"

2 Different Views of Old Testament Commands Quoted in the New Testament	
Reformed, Covenant Theology	New Covenant Theology
Continued	Transferred

Covenant theologians often reason, "Since Old Testament commands are quoted in the New Testament, therefore they're still binding."

That's one possibility. The other possibility is that Old Testament commands quoted in the New Testament have been transferred, reinstated, and canonized into the New Covenant canon (the New Testament). To simplify it, let's just say they were transferred.

> **Old Testament commands quoted in the New Testament have been transferred.**

Doug Moo seems to believe the transfer view when he says that Christ "takes up" into His teaching some of Moses' commands...

> "...we see Mosaic commandments taken up into and made part of the 'law of Christ'...Yes, Christ 'ends' the reign of the law, imposing his own law 'in place of' the law of Moses. But in doing so, the New Testament stresses, he both brings that law to its intended conclusion and goal and also takes up within his own teaching and reapplies to his followers portions of that law."[17]

This transfer view fits well with the understanding that the whole law of Moses is cancelled. It also fits well with the archaeological discovery that our Bible consists of 2 distinct canons: The Old Covenant canon (Old Testament) and the New Covenant canon

---

[17] Moo in Gundry, 315.

(New Testament). (See more on the archaeology of the covenants from Meredith Kline in #17 below.)

Example of a Law Transferred From
An Old Contract to a New Contract

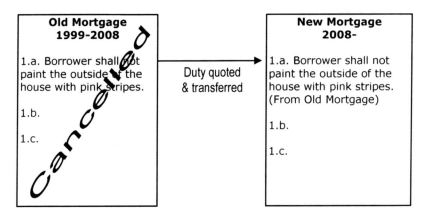

Suppose a couple has a mortgage on their house. And, that mortgage has a clause stating, "Borrower shall not paint the outside of the house with pink stripes."

Next, imagine they hear an ad that mortgage rates are dropping. So, they call their original lender and ask to refinance the mortgage. And, the lender quotes and transfers that clause from the old mortgage to the new mortgage, "Borrower shall not paint the outside of the house with pink stripes."

Finally, suppose they're feeling rebellious, so they decide to paint their house with pink stripes.

Now, here's the question: Which mortgage did they violate?

    1. The old mortgage?
    2. Both mortgages?
    3. The new mortgage?

Obviously, they violated only the new mortgage, since the old mortgage contract was completely cancelled, and superceded by the new mortgage contract. And, some clauses were transferred from the old contract to the new contract.

Do you see the analogy from the old and new mortgages to the Old and New Covenants? (Also, try this analogy with any type of contract, like 2 car leases.)

Likewise, the Old and New Covenants contain 2 contracts. So, a Christian who stole, violated Ephesians 4:28, not Exodus 20:15. And, a Christian who dishonored his father and mother, violated Ephesians 6:2, not Exodus 20:12. (Remember "The 30-Second, Law-View Test" earlier?)

Jesus Christ and His apostles transferred many commands from the Old Covenant to the New Covenant. Plus, they also gave several, new commands not previously revealed in the Old Covenant.

9. "But That's Just Dispensationalism"

When some Covenant Theologians hear the view that all Old Testament laws are cancelled, they protest, "But, that's just Dispensationalism!"

However, isn't their view that the so-called "ceremonial and civil laws" are cancelled also "Dispensationalism?" You see, all Christians are "Dispensational" on the law of Moses: Covenant Theology on 1/3 - 2/3, and New Covenant Theology on 3/3. Now I ask you, "Who is more consistent?"

So far, we've seen 9 objections (including 5 misinterpreted verses) by Covenant Theology. Those who still insist on believing in Covenant Theology remind me of evolutionists. Where is the proof? Where are the verses that prove...

1. One covenant of grace, as opposed to multiple covenants?
2. The law of Moses can be divided into 3 parts?
3. The Ten Commandments = the eternal, unchanging moral law of God?
4. The Sabbath was changed from Saturday to Sunday?

Those 4, key foundations to Covenant Theology are based on mere presuppositions, not explicit verses. Covenant theology is really "Old Covenant Theology." On the other hand, New Covenant Theology bases its main foundations on explicit verses.

> **"Covenant Theology is really Old Covenant Theology."**

Part II.
8 Reasons Why All Old Testament Laws Are Cancelled

10. The Decalogue Is the Foundational Document of the Whole Old Covenant

Remember from #1 earlier, that God calls the Ten Commandments "the covenant" in 4 verses?

> "He wrote on the tablets *the words of the covenant, the Ten Commandments"* (Ex. 34:28).

> "And He declared to you *His covenant* which He commanded you to perform, *the Ten Commandments..."* (Deut. 4:13).

> "And there I have provided a place for *the ark, in which is the covenant* of the LORD that he made with our fathers when he brought them out of the land of Egypt" (1 Kings 8:21).

> "And there I have set *the ark, in which is the covenant* of the LORD that he made with the people of Israel" (2 Chr. 6:11).

The Old Covenant is the "Decalogue-Covenant." Notice in the last 2 verses who God made the Decalogue-Covenant with: Israel (not us Gentiles).

"The Old Covenant is the "Decalogue-Covenant."

These verses don't say that the Ten Commandments are the *whole* Old Covenant. But, they do say the Ten Commandments are the Old Covenant. Therefore, you must believe that the Ten Commandments are the Old Covenant in at least some sense, right?

The Old Covenant can not be reduced to only the Decalogue. Nor can it be reduced to only the so-called "civil and ceremonial laws." The whole Old Covenant included the Decalogue, "civil, and ceremonial laws." Therefore, when the Old Covenant was cancelled, the Decalogue, "civil, and ceremonial laws" were cancelled.

(To understand more about how the Decalogue functioned in redemptive history read *Tablets of Stone and the History of Redemption* by John Reisinger.)

11. The Law of Moses Can't Be Divided Into 3 Parts

Did Paul really believe that the law of Moses could be divided into 3-parts: Moral, civil, and ceremonial?

The 3-Part, Division of the Law
Invented by a 13th-Century, Roman Catholic?

Richard Barcellos, a Reformed Baptist, Covenant Theologian, concedes what I've heard elsewhere: The 3-part, division of the law can be traced back to Thomas Aquinas, the 13th-century, Roman Catholic philosopher-theologian...

"1. The History of the Three-Fold Division of the Law
The three-fold division of the law into moral, ceremonial, and judicial is not unique to Calvin. By the time of Calvin, it was common to divide the law into these three divisions. According to Hesselink, this paradigm goes back to Aquinas. (Hesselink, *Calvin's Concept of the Law*, 102)."[18]

Barcellos is probably correct since Aquinas distinguishes 3 parts of the law in his famous *Summa Theologica*...

"We must therefore distinguish three kinds of precept in the Old Law; viz. "moral" precepts, which are dictated by the natural law; "ceremonial" precepts, which are determinations of the Divine worship; and "judicial" precepts, which are determinations of the justice to be maintained among men. Wherefore the Apostle (Romans 7:12) after saying that the "Law is holy," adds that "the commandment is just, and holy, and good": "just," in respect of the judicial precepts; "holy," with regard to the ceremonial precepts (since the word "sanctus"--"holy"--is applied to that which is consecrated to God); and "good," i.e. conducive to virtue, as to the moral precepts."[19]

---

[18] Richard Barcellos, "Calvin on the Three-Fold Division of the Law" *Midwest Center for Theological Studies Blog,* 11/5/07, mctsowensboro.org/blog/?p=231)

[19] Thomas Aquinas, "Question 99: Article 4, "The Precepts of the Old Law," in *The Summa Theologica of St. Thomas Aquinas,* Second and Revised Edition, 1920, Online Edition, 2006, www.newadvent.org/summa/2099.htm

So, when Paul made all those negative statements about the law, he could not possibly have meant "only the civil and ceremonial law, but not the moral law," since that view wasn't even invented until 1200 years after he wrote.

The Reformers carried some extra baggage out of Rome, namely the 3-part division of the law of Moses into moral, civil, and ceremonial. Plus, the Reformers borrowed Rome's practices of infant baptism and state-Church theocracy.

(Also, did you know that the orthodox, Jewish rabbis in Jerusalem deny that the law can be divided into moral, civil, and ceremonial parts?)

Scripture makes a distinction between the Ten Commandments, and the rest of the law. But, the distance between distinction and division is as wide as the Grand Canyon.

And, Scripture ranks a couple duties from the law as "more important" than others (Mk. 12:28-31) and "weightier" than others (Mt. 23:23). But, the difference between importance and division is as big as Mt. Everest.

Contrary to Covenant Theology, 3 verses show the unity of the whole law of Moses...

> "...Cursed be everyone who does not abide by *all things* written in the book of the law and do them" (Gal. 3:10).

> "...every man who accepts circumcision that he is obligated to keep *the whole law*" (Gal. 5:3).

> "For whoever keeps *the whole law, but fails in one point, has become accountable for all of it*" (James 2:10).

Paul and James knew that the law was one, indivisible, whole covenant. They could not possibly imagine that only part of it (the Decalogue) could still be in force after Christ.

12. The Apostles Never Made Exceptions Qualifying Their Criticisms of the Whole Law of Moses

When teaching about the law, the apostles made several positive statements and several negative statements. We dealt with Covenant Theology's misinterpretation of the positive statements in Part I. But, they also misinterpret the negative statements.

Covenant Theology would have us believe that when the apostles criticized the law, what they really meant was part of the law, not all of it. But, as we saw in #11 above, the law of Moses can't be separated into 3, self-existent parts. (Some Covenant Theologians interpret Paul's negative statements against the law as referring to the curse of the law or legalism.)

Covenant Theology Reads Exceptions Into All the Negative Verses on the Law

The apostles never once made exceptions or qualifications to their criticisms of the law. Yet, some Covenant Theologians read the following exceptions and qualifications into all these criticisms of the law...

"by placing *(part of the law)* a yoke *(except the Ten Commandments)* on the neck of the disciples that neither our fathers nor we have been able to bear?" (Acts 15:10).

"...lay on you no greater burden than these requirements *(and the Ten Commandments)*" (Acts 15:28).

"...the law is binding on a person only as long as he lives...you also have died to the law through the body of Christ...But now we are released from the law, having died to that which held us captive, so that we should serve not under the old written code *(except the Ten Commandments)* but in the new life of the Spirit" (Rom. 7:1-6; cf. Gal. 2:19).

"...the law was our guardian until Christ came...we are no longer under a guardian *(except the Ten Commandments)...*" (Gal. 3:24-25).

"Tell me, you who desire to be under the law...Mount Sinai bearing children for slavery...'Cast out the slave woman and her son' *(except the Ten Commandments)*...do not submit again to a yoke of slavery" (Gal. 4:21-5:1).

"But if you are led by the Spirit, you are not under the law *(except the Ten Commandments)*...against such things there is no law" (Gal. 5:18-23).

"by abolishing *(part of)* the law of commandments and ordinances *(except the Ten Commandments)...* " (Eph. 2:15).

"...having forgiven you all trespasses, having wiped out the handwriting of requirements *(except the Ten Commandments)* that was against us, which was contrary to us. And He has taken it out of the way, having nailed it to the cross" (NKJV, Col. 2:13-14).

"For when there is a change in the priesthood there is necessarily change in *(part of)* the law *(except the Ten Commandments)* as well" (Heb. 7:12).

The natural interpretation of "the law" is "the whole law," not "part of the law." Isn't it unthinkable that a Jewish author like Paul intended to preserve the Decalogue when he criticized the whole law without making any exceptions for it?

13. Since Genesis Is Part of the Law, the Commands From Genesis – Sinai Are Cancelled

Did you know that Genesis is part of the law as revelation (Old Testament?) Here are 4 reasons showing why Genesis is part of the law...

1. Genesis 21 is called "the law" in Galatians 4:21-22.

> "Tell me, you who desire to be under the law, *do you not listen to the law?* For it is written that Abraham had two sons: one by a slave woman and one by a free woman" (Gal. 4:21-22 referring to Gen. 21; cf. Rom. 3:31ff.)

2. The phrase "law and prophets" means "Genesis–Malachi" (the whole Old Testament).

3. Moses wrote the book of Genesis.

4. Archaeology testifies that Genesis is the historical introduction to the Old Covenant canon. God patterned the Old Covenant's literary structure with some similarities to ancient, near-Eastern treaties, which included an historical introduction before the actual covenant document.

Ancient covenants were put into effect with a surrounding body of literature, a.k.a. canon. Covenant produces canon. Our Bible is made of 2 major covenants, the Old and New covenants, each surrounded by its own canon, the Old and New Testaments.

(To understand this more, see *The Structure of Biblical Authority* in #17 below...)

So, when the New Testament says the law is cancelled, that includes Genesis, not just post-Sinai commands.

14. The Jerusalem Council Concluded That Gentile Converts Don't Need to Obey the Law of Moses for Justification or Sanctification

Many years ago, I clearly remember hearing a well-known, Covenant Theologian concede that he didn't understand Acts 15. Of course he didn't understand it. What he meant was that he didn't understand how it could possibly fit it into his system of Covenant Theology.

The Jerusalem Council met for the express purpose of determining whether Gentile converts had to keep the law of Moses to be "saved." The word "saved" includes past justification, present sanctification, and future glorification, not merely justification (a common view among Arminians and Fundamentalists).

The text clearly shows that the meeting agenda included sanctification...

> "But some of the believers who belonged to the party of the Pharisees rose up and said, "It is necessary to circumcise them *and to order them to keep the law of Moses.* The apostles and the elders were gathered together to consider this matter" (Acts 15:5-6).

> "For it has seemed good to the Holy Spirit and to us to lay on you no greater burden than *these requirements* (for sanctification, not justification): that you abstain from what has been sacrificed to idols, and from blood, and from what has been strangled, and from sexual immorality..." (Acts 15:28-29).

> "...they delivered to them *the decrees to keep* (for sanctification, not justification)" (Acts 16:4).

> "(But) as for the Gentiles *who have believed (already justified),* we have sent a letter with our judgment that they should abstain from what has been sacrificed to idols, and from blood, and from what has been strangled, and from sexual immorality" (Acts 21:25).

Clearly, those 4 commands were given for sanctification, not justification. The apostles intentionally omitted the Sabbath and the Decalogue for Gentile converts' sanctification. No doubt, the apostles weren't Sabbatarians or Covenant Theologians.

So, the issue is, "Must Gentile converts keep the law of Moses for salvation (both justification and sanctification)?" If you asked that question to a Covenant Theologian today, how would he answer? He would reply in a heartbeat, "The ceremonial and civil laws have passed away, but the Ten Commandments are still binding."

But, the apostles never gave that defense of the Decalogue or Sabbath because it wasn't invented until the 13th century. If ever there was an opportunity for the apostles to teach that the Decalogue and Sabbath are binding on Gentile converts, this was it! Instead, they defended salvation (justification and sanctification) by God's grace, through faith, without works from the law of Moses.

In Acts 15, the Holy Spirit even calls the whole law of Moses (including the Decalogue) "a yoke"...

> "Now, therefore, why are you putting God to the test by placing *a yoke* on the neck of the disciples that neither our fathers nor we have been able to bear?" (Acts 15:10).

> "...two covenants. One is from Mount Sinai...do not submit again to a *yoke of slavery"* (Gal. 4:24, 5:1).

But, look at the contrast between the law of Moses vs. the law of Christ...

> "Come to me, all who labor and are heavy burdened, and I will give you rest. Take my yoke upon you, and learn from me, for I am gentle and lowly in heart, and you will find rest for your souls. *For my yoke is easy, and my burden is light.* At that time Jesus went through the grain fields on the Sabbath" (Mt. 11:28-12:1).

> "...And his commandments are *not burdensome"* (1 Jn. 5:3).

And, see the sharp contrast between Paul's law observance vs. the Gentile believers...

> *"...you yourself (Paul) also live in observance of the law. (But) as for the Gentiles who have believed,* we have sent a letter with our judgment that they should abstain from what has been sacrificed to idols, and from blood, and from what has been strangled, and from sexual immorality" (Acts 21:24-25).

God was revealing a new canon (rule) for His Church (just like He did for Adam and Eve, and the patriarchs). The Church's canon started with Christ's oral teaching, then the apostles' oral teaching, the prophets' prophecies, and finally the writing of the New Testament books. This is the Church's new foundation, built in the 1st century (Eph. 2:19-20ff., cf. 3:5, 4:11).

15. The Whole Decalogue Had an Historical Beginning and End

In the book *Tablets of Stone and the History of Redemption*, John Reisinger observes that the whole law of Moses, including the Decalogue as the Old Covenant document, had a historical beginning.

Granted, 9 of the Ten Commandments may have been in force as conscience law before Sinai. But, it was not until Sinai, that God combined them together with the Sabbath-sign into the Ten Commandments...

> *"Not with our fathers (Abraham) did the LORD make this covenant..."* (Deut. 5:3; cf. Ex. 34:28; Deut. 4:13; 1 Kings 8:21; 1 Chr. 6:11).

> "He declared His word to Jacob, His statutes and rules to Israel. *He has not dealt thus with any other (Gentile) nation;* they do not know his rules" (Ps. 147:19-20).

> *"...before the law was given* (~1446 B.C.)..." (Rom. 5:13).

> *"Moreover the law entered* (~1446 B.C.)..." (Rom. 5:20).

> *"(the law) was added* (~1446 B.C.) because of transgressions, *until the Seed* should come..." (Gal. 3:19).

And, the whole law of Moses including the Decalogue as the Old Covenant document had a historical end. Granted, 9 of the Ten Commandments may be transferred into the New Covenant, law of Christ. But they are no longer combined into one, whole document...

> "having forgiven us all our trespasses, *having wiped out the handwriting (Ten Commandments) of requirements that was against us,* which was contrary to us. And He has taken it out of the way, having nailed it to the cross" (NKJV, Col. 2:13-14; cf. Ex. 32:16).

"by abolishing the law of commandments and ordinances..." (Eph. 2:15).

"...God, who has made us competent to be ministers of a new covenant, not of the letter but of the Spirit. For the letter kills, but the Spirit gives life. Now if *the ministry of death, carved in letters on stone...the ministry of condemnation...For if what was being brought to an end came with glory..."* (2 Cor. 3:5-9).

"Why then the law? It was added because of transgressions, *until the Offspring (~30 A.D.) should come..."* (Gal. 3:19).

"...the law was our guardian *until Christ came (~30 A.D.),* in order that we might be justified by faith. But now that faith has come, we are *no longer under a guardian"* (Gal. 3:24-25).

"In speaking of a New Covenant, He makes the first one obsolete. And what is becoming obsolete and growing old is *ready to vanish away...the tablets of the covenant"* (Heb. 8:13 - 9:4).

"For you have not come to (Mt. Sinai)..." (Heb. 12:18ff.)

What this means is that there was no whole Decalogue in force before Sinai (from creation to ~1446 B.C.) or after the cross (~30 A.D.) The Decalogue had an historical beginning in ~1446 B.C. – and an historical end in ~30 A.D. So, the Decalogue was in force only temporarily.

16. The Church Is Built on the Foundation of New Testament Apostles and Prophets' Teaching

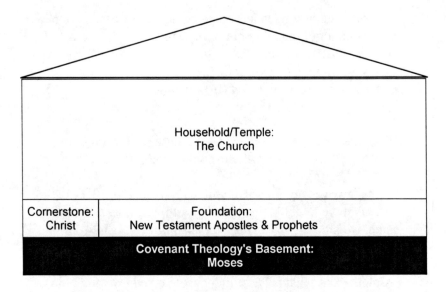

"...the household of God, *built on the foundation of the apostles and prophets,* Christ Jesus Himself being the cornerstone" (Eph. 2:19-20ff., cf. 3:5, 4:11).

"For in Christ Jesus...*a new creation. And as for all who walk by this rule...*" (Gk. "kanon", Gal. 6:15-16).

Many interpreters wrongly assume that Ephesians 2:19-20 is speaking of New Testament apostles and Old Testament prophets. But, by cross-referencing that passage with the "apostles and prophets" in Ephesians 3:5 and 4:11, Paul clearly means "New Testament prophets," not "Old Testament prophets." Also, notice that Paul's order is apostles first, then prophets second.

So Paul is saying, "The church of God is built on the foundation of the New Covenant apostles and prophets, with Christ as the cornerstone." In other words, the Church is a new, redemptive-historical creation built on the new revelation of the apostles and prophets in the 1st century.

Of course, Old Testament saints were transferred into the Church after it's creation in the 1st century. But, the relation of the assembly/congregation of Israel to the New Testament Church is only that of type - antitype, not equality. Israel was like the Church in some ways, but Israel ≠ the Church in all ways.

Notice Paul's construction analogy, and its order...

> 1st: The cornerstone (Jesus Christ) was placed in the 1st century.
> 2nd: The foundation (apostles and prophets) was laid in the 1st century.
> 3rd: The building (the Church) is being built from the 1st century – the end.

Covenant Theology tries to make Moses a basement below the foundation. But, that's a house built on an unstable foundation.

17. Archaeology Testifies That the Bible Contains 2 Separate Canons (Rules)

Scholars generally agree that archaeology shows God patterned the Old Covenant's literary structure with several similarities to ancient, near-Eastern treaties.

Ancient covenants were put into effect with a surrounding body of literature, or canon. (Genesis is structured as the historical introduction to the Old Covenant.) Covenant produces canon.

Our Bible is made of 2 major covenants, the Old and New Covenants, each surrounded by its own canon, the Old and New Testaments. Meredith Kline sums it up well in *The Structure of Biblical Authority...*

Two Covenants Implies 2 Canons

"In fact, if biblical canon is *covenantal canon* and there are in the composition of the Bible two covenants, one old and one new, there are also *two canons, one old and one new. Instead of speaking of the canon of Scripture, we should then speak of the Old and New Testament canons,* or of the canonical covenants which constitute the Scripture...*the old and new covenant canons...* The identity of *the Old and New Testaments as two distinct canons* and the integrity of *each Testament in itself as a separate canonical whole...the two covenantal canons...* "[20]

Two Testaments Implies 2 Canon Rules

"...*the two Testaments which serve as community rules for the two orders...they are two discrete canons in series...two treaty canons, old and new, within the church's Scriptures*"[21]

The Old Testament Canon Does Not Govern the Church

"This is to say that *the Old Testament is not the canon of the*

---

[20] Kline, 97.
[21] Kline, 99, 110.

Christian church... the Old Testament, though possessing the general authority of all the Scriptures, does not possess for the church the more specific authority of canonicity. Under the new covenant, *the Old Testament is not the current canon.* "[22]

The New Testament Canon Governs the Church

"...*the treaty canon that governs the Church of the new covenant as a formal community is the New Testament alone,* while Scripture is the broader entity...the Old and New Testaments together....*the New Testament canon is the currently normative canon for the church*... "[23]

It sounds like he is saying that the New Covenant is not an addendum, codicil, P.S., or rider added onto the Old Covenant. The New Covenant is a separate covenant, with a separate canon (rule).

> **"...the New Covenant is not an addendum, codicil, P.S., or rider added onto the Old Covenant."**

The Old and New Covenants contain contract duties. The old contract was cancelled. The new contract is in force. Our duties are defined by the covenant that we're under. We're under the New Covenant, not the Old Covenant. Therefore, our duties are defined by the New Covenant.

Now, it's time to summarize what we've learned so far about Covenant Theology. Let's compare the Bible to the Covenant Theology in the *Westminster Confession of Faith* (W.C.F.) and the *Westminster Shorter Catechism* (W.S.C.) Keep in mind that the W.C.F.'s Covenant Theology is almost identical to that in the *Second London Baptist Confession of Faith of 1689.*

---

[22] Kline, 99, 102.
[23] Kline, 100-101, 107.

Comparison Chart of Covenant Theology vs. The Word of God	
The Canons	
One Canon	**Two Canons**
"...the books of the Old & New Testament_..." (W.C.F. 1:2). "...All which are...the rule_ of faith & life" (W.C.F. 1:2). "...the canon_ of Scripture..." (W.C.F. 1:3). (Notice the singulars instead of plurals.)	"...the household of God (the Church), *built on the foundation of the (N.T.) apostles & prophets,* Christ Jesus Himself being the cornerstone" (Eph. 2:19-20ff., cf. 3:5, 4:11). "...a new creation. And as all for who walk by this rule..." (Gk. "kanon" the rule of the new creation, Gal. 6:15-16).
The Covenants	
Before the Fall, God Made a Covenant of Works With Adam, Promising Life if He Obeyed	**Adam Already Possessed Spiritual Life, So He Didn't Have to Earn It**
"...a covenant of works, wherein life was promised to Adam..." (W.C.F. 7:2, cf. 19:1).	"You may surely eat of *every tree* (including the tree of life) of the garden, but of the tree of the knowledge of good and evil you shall not eat, for in the day that you eat of it you shall surely (spiritually) *die* (of the life you already possess)" (Gen. 2:16).
After the Fall, God Made a Covenant of Grace With Adam	**God Spoke a Curse to Satan, (Not a Covenant of Grace to Adam)**
"...the Lord was pleased to make a second (with Adam), commonly called the covenant of grace..." (W.C.F. 7:3).	*1. "The LORD God said to the serpent...cursed are you...I will put enmity between you and the woman, and between your

	offspring and her offspring; He shall bruise *your* head (serpent, not Adam), & *you* (serpent, not Adam) shall bruise His heel" (Gen. 3:14-15). *2. "To the woman He said* (cursed)..." (Gen. 3:16). *3. "And to Adam He said* (cursed)..." (Gen. 3:17).
The Old Covenant Was The Covenant of Grace "This covenant of grace...was administered by promises, prophecies, sacrifices, circumcision, the paschal lamb, and other types and ordinances delivered to the people of the Jews..." (W.C.F. 7:4-5).	**The Old Covenant's Nature & Terms Were Conditional, Works (But it Was Motivated by God's Gracious Purpose)** "...the righteousness that is based on the law, that the person who does the commandments shall live by them. *But* the righteousness based on faith..." (Rom. 10:5-6). *"But the law is not of faith,* rather 'The one who does them shall live by them'" (Gal. 3:12).
One Covenant "...There are not therefore two covenants of grace differing in substance, but one & the same, under various dispensations" (W.C.F. 7:6).	**Separate, Multiple Covenants** "...Israelites, and to them belong...*the covenants...*" (Rom. 9:4). "who has made us competent to be ministers of a *New Covenant...*" (2 Cor. 3:6). "...*the covenantS* of promise..." (Eph. 2:12).

	"...these women are *two covenants...*" (Gal. 4:24). "*...first covenant...a second*" (Heb. 8:7). "*...a New Covenant...NOT like the covenant that I made with their fathers* in the day when I took them by the hand to bring them out of the land of Egypt..." (Heb. 8:8-9). "In speaking of *a New Covenant,* He makes *the first one* obsolete..." (Heb. 8:13). "...Jesus, the Mediator *of a New Covenant...*" (Heb. 12:24).
The Law of God	
The Law of Moses Can Be Divided Into 3 Separate Parts	**The Law of Moses Is One, Unified Whole**
"Besides this law, commonly called moral...ceremonial laws...judicial laws..." (W.C.F. 19:3-4).	"Cursed be everyone who does not abide by *all things written in the book of the Law,* and do them" (Gal. 3:10). "...every man who accepts circumcision that he is obligated to keep *the whole law*" (Gal. 5:3). "...for whoever keeps the whole *law* but fails in one point has become accountable for *all of it*" (Jas. 2:10).

The Sins of the Gentiles Defined by the Ten Commandments	The Sins of the Gentiles Defined Apart From the Ten Commandments
"The moral law doth for ever bind all, as well justified persons as others, to the obedience thereof..." (W.C.F. 19:5).	"For the wrath of God is revealed from Heaven against all ungodliness and unright-eousness of men, who by their unrighteousness suppress the truth. For what can be known about God is plain to them..." (Rom. 1:18-32; 1 Cor. 6:9-10; Gal. 5:19-21; Rev. 21:8, 22:15).
The Ten Commandments Are the Eternal, Unchanging, Moral Law of God	**The Ten Commandments Are the Old Covenant's Foundational Document**
"The moral law is summarily comprehended in the ten commandments" (W.S.C., A. 41).	"...He wrote on the tablets *the words of the covenant, the Ten Commandments"* (Ex. 34:28). *"...His covenant which He commanded you to perform, that is the Ten Commandments..."* (Deut. 4:13). *"...the ark, in which is the covenant..."* (1 Kings 8:21; cf. 1 Chr. 6:11).
God Gave Adam the Ten Commandments at Creation	**The Whole Old Covenant, Law of Moses (Incl. the Decalogue) Began at Sinai**
"God gave to Adam a law...in ten commandments..." (W.C.F. 19:1-2).	*"Not with our fathers did the LORD make this covenant (a.k.a. Decalogue),* but with us...today" (Deut. 5:3; cf. Ex. 34:28; Deut. 4:13; 1 Kings 8:21; 1 Chr. 6:11).

	"He revealed His word to Jacob, His statutes and His judgments to Israel. *He has not done so with any nation; and they have not known his judgments"* (Ps. 147:19-20). *"...before the law was given,* but sin is not counted *when there is no law"* (Rom. 5:13). "...the law *entered..."* (NKJV, Rom. 5:20). "...(the law) *was added* because of transgressions, until the offspring should come..." (Gal. 3:19).
The Ten Commandments Are Still Binding on Us Today "The moral law doth for ever bind all..." (W.C.F. 19:5).	**The Whole Decalogue Ended in the 1st Century and Is No Longer Binding Today** "...lay on you *no greater burden than these..."* (Acts 15:28). "...you yourself (Paul) also live in observance of *the law. (But) as for the Gentiles* who have believed..." (Acts 21:24-25). *"...you are not under law* but under grace" (Rom. 6:14; cf. Jn. 1:17). "...the law is binding on a person only as long as he lives...you also have *died to the law* through the body of Christ...But now we are released from the law, having died to that

which held us captive, so that we serve not under the old written code but in the new life of the Spirit" (Rom. 7:1-6; cf. Gal. 2:19).

"not on tablets of stone...the ministry of death (and con-demnation), carved in letters on stone..." (2 Cor. 3:3-9).

"Why then the law? It was added because of transgressions, *until* the offspring should come..." (Gal. 3:19).

"...the law was our guardian *until* Christ came...*we are no longer under a guardian"* (Gal. 3:24-25).

"...under guardians & managers until the date set by the father... enslaved to the elementary principles of the world...weak & worthless elementary principles of the world whose slaves you want to be..." (Gal. 4:2, 3, 9).

"...you who desire to be under the law...Mount Sinai bearing children for slavery...*'Cast out the slave woman & her son'*...do not submit again to a yoke of slavery" (Gal. 4:21-5:1).

"But if you are led by the Spirit, *you are not under the law*... against such things there is no law..." (Gal. 5:18-23).

	"by abolishing the law of commandments & ordinances..." (Eph. 2:15). "...having forgiven you *all trespasses, having wiped out the handwriting of requirements that was against us,* which was contrary to us. And He has taken it out of the way, having nailed it to the cross" (Col. 2:13-14, NKJV). "...the law is not laid down for the just, but for the lawless..." (1 Tim. 1:9). "For when there is a change in the priesthood, there is necessarily *a change in the law"* (Heb. 7:12). "...what is becoming obsolete & growing old is ready to vanish away...*the tablets of the covenant"* (Heb. 8:13-9:4). *"For you have not come to (Mt. Sinai)..."* (Heb. 12:18ff.).
The Law of Christ W.C.F.?	**The Law of Christ** "...the coastlands will wait for *His (My Servant's) law"* (Is. 42:4). "...not being outside the law of God, but *(Gk.: in-lawed) to Christ..."* (1 Cor. 9:21).

	"...fulfill the law of Christ" (Gal. 6:2). "For My yoke is easy & My burden is light" (Mt. 11:30; cf. Acts 15:10; Gal. 5:1; 1 Jn. 5:3). "teaching them to *observe all that I have commanded you...*" (Mt. 28:20). "If you love Me, you will *keep My commandments"* (Jn. 14:15; cf. 14:21-24, 15:10). *"...what instructions we gave you through the Lord Jesus"* (1 Thes. 4:2). "...we know (Him), if we *keep His commandments"* (1 Jn. 2:3).
The Sabbath	
Holy Times "...a due proportion of time be set apart for the worship of God..." (W.C.F. 21:7).	**Worship God Always (24/7), Not During "Holy Times" Only** "...they ought *always* to pray..." (Lk. 18:1; cf. Eph. 6:18; 1 Th. 5:17). "giving thanks *always...* " (Eph. 5:20). "...present your bodies as a *living* sacrifice..." (Rom. 12:1). "So, whether you eat or drink, or *whatever you do,* do all to the glory of God" (1 Cor. 10:31).

	"...let us *continually* offer up a sacrifice of praise to God" (Heb. 13:15).
One Day in Seven "...He hath particularly appointed one day in seven..." (W.C.F. 21:7).	**The Sabbath Was the 7th Day, Not One Day in Seven** "...on *the seventh day,* which is a Sabbath..." (Ex. 16:26). "...*the seventh day* is a Sabbath to the LORD your God...the LORD blessed the Sabbath day & made it holy" (Ex. 20:10-11).
God Gave Adam The Sabbath at Creation "...a Sabbath...from the beginning of the world..." (W.C.F. 21:7).	**God First Revealed & Gave The 24-Hour, Weekly Sabbath To Israel in the Wilderness, Not Adam at Creation** "So I led them out of the land of Egypt and brought them into the wilderness...I *gave* them my Sabbaths..." (Ezek. 20:10, 12). "You came down on Mount Sinai...and you *made known* to them your holy Sabbath..." (Neh. 9:13-14).
The Sabbath Was Changed From Saturday to Sunday "...a Sabbath, to be kept holy unto him: which, from the beginning of the world to the resurrection of Christ, was the last day of the week: and, from the resurrection of Christ, was changed into the first day of the week..." (W.C.F. 21:7).	**The Literal Greek for "the First Day of the Week" Is "the First (Day) From The Sabbath"** "...first (day) from the Sabbath..." (Gk: mia sabbaton, or protos Sabbaton in Mt. 28:1; Mk. 16:2, 16:9; Lk. 24:1; Jn. 20:1, 20:19; Acts 20:7; 1 Cor. 16:2; cf. Acts 13:14, 13:27,

	13:42, 13:44, 15:21, 16:13, 17:1-2, 18:4).
The Lord's Day = the Sabbath "…in Scripture is called the Lord's Day…" (W.C.F. 21:7).	**No Biblical Evidence That Lord's Day = Sabbath** "I was in the Spirit on the Lord's Day…" (Rev. 1:10, cf. 4:2, 7:3, 21:10).
The Sabbath Is Still Binding Today "…and is to be continued to the end of the world, as the Christian Sabbath" (W.C.F. 21:7).	**The Weekly Sabbath Is:** **1. An issue of personal liberty** **2. Weak and worthless** **3. A shadow fulfilled by Christ** "One person esteems one *day* as better than another, while another esteems all *days* alike. Each one should be fully convinced in his own mind" (Rom. 14:5). "…how can you turn back again to the *weak and worthless* elementary principles of the world, whose slaves you want to be once more? *You observe days* and months and seasons and years!" (Gal. 4:9-10). "Therefore let no one pass judgment on you in questions of food and drink, or with regard to a festival, or a new moon or *Sabbath(s). These are a shadow of the things to come, but the substance belongs to Christ"* (Col 2:16-17; cf. Ezek. 45:17; Hos. 2:11; 1 Chr. 23:31; 2 Chr. 31:3; Lev. 23:2-44).

| The Sign of the Old Covenant

W.C.F.? | The Sign of the Old Covenant
Was the Sabbath

"...Above all you shall keep my Sabbaths, for this is a *sign* between Me and you...Therefore the people of Israel shall keep the Sabbath, observing the Sabbath throughout their generations, *as a covenant forever. It is a sign...* " (Ex. 31:13, 16-17).

"Moreover, I gave them My Sabbaths, as a *sign* between Me and them...keep My Sabbaths holy that they may be a sign between Me and you..." (Ezek. 20:12, 20). |
| God's Eternal Sabbath Rest

W.C.F.? | We Enter Into God's Eternal Sabbath Rest by Believing the Gospel

"For good news came to us...For we who have believed enter that rest..." (Heb. 4:2-3). |

If I'm right in the above chart on Covenant Theology vs. the Word of God, then there are at least 16 errors (plus infant baptism) in the *Westminster Confession.* And, the *1689 Baptist Confession* shares many of the same errors.

There's much we can learn from the famous, Reformed confessions. But, only God's Word is inspired and inerrant. "Sola Scriptura."

Part III.
3 Objections to
"All New Testament Laws Are for Our Obedience"

God justifies us freely by His grace through faith in Jesus Christ. So, we don't work to be justified. But, after He has justified us, by His grace we do good works while growing in Christ.

What is Antinomianism? It means "against law." Who is an Antinomian? For our purposes, we will define a doctrinal Antinomian as anyone who does not love (Ps. 119), and teach (Mt. 28:20) God's commands. Doctrinal Antinomians may be fuzzy on their definitions of law and sin, but still obey God's commands. (A practical Antinomian does not obey God's commands, and thus is unregenerate.)

This brand of Antinomianism is rare among scholars. It's more commonly found in the pews and discussion forums. Here are 3 common objections by some Antinomians...

18. "But We're Not Under Law, But Under Grace"

Yes, we're not under law, but under grace. But, what does that mean? (By the way, the Bible never contrasts law and gospel. But, it contrasts law and grace twice.) Here are the 2 key passages...

"Do not present your members to sin as instruments for unrighteousness, but present yourselves to God as those who have been brought from death to life, and your members to God as instruments for righteousness. For sin will have no dominion over you, since *you are not under law but under grace.* What then? Are we to sin because *we are not under law but under grace?* By no means! Do you not know that if you present yourselves to anyone as obedient slaves, you are slaves of the one whom you obey, either of sin, which leads to death, or of obedience, which leads to righteousness?" (Rom. 6:14-15).

"And from his fullness we have all received, grace upon grace. For *the law was given through Moses; grace and truth came through Jesus Christ"* (Jn. 1:16).

What do those 2 passages tell us about law and grace? Here are 3 clear facts about law and grace...

1. The relationship between law and grace is a contrast, not a comparison. (See the word "but" in Rom. 6.)

2. In John 1:16, law and grace refer to 2 different times in redemptive history: Law was from the time of Moses – Christ (~1445 B.C. - 30 A.D.) and grace is from the time of Christ – the end (~30 A.D. - the end). Therefore, not under law, but under grace refers to *redemption accomplished* for the corporate Church in the 1st century, not the time of Moses.

3. In Rom. 6:14, law and grace refer to 2 different lifestyles: sin vs. obedience. (Most in Israel were characterized by sin, but all in the Church are characterized by obedience.) Therefore, not under law, but under grace also refers to *redemption applied* to individuals in the 1st - 21st centuries.

Some historic Dispensationalists believed there was no grace during the time of law. But, that view is easily disproved by a simple, concordance topical word study...

"But Noah found *grace* in the eyes of the LORD" (Gen. 6:8).

"...you (Moses) have found *grace* in My sight" (Ex. 33:12).

"Toward the scorners He is scornful, but to the humble He gives *grace*" (Prov. 3:34).

And, some modern Antinomians believe there is no law during the time of grace. However, that view is also easily disproved from a concordance...

"Bear one another's burdens, and so fulfill the *law of Christ*" (Gal. 6:2).

"I will put my *laws* into their minds, and write them on their hearts..." (Heb. 8:10).

"He will bring forth justice to the nations...coastlands shall wait for *His law*" (Is. 42:1, 4).

"Go therefore and make disciples of all nations, baptizing them...teaching them to *observe all that I have commanded you....*" (Mt. 28:19-20; cf. Jn. 14:15, 14:21, 15:10; Acts 1:2; 1 Th. 4:2; 1 Cor. 7:19; 1 Jn. 2:3, 3:22, 3:24, 5:2-3; 2 Jn. 6; Rev. 12:17).

Therefore, just as there was grace during the time of law, so there is law during the time of grace. There are grace and truth in the Old Testament, and law in the New Testament. Whatever it means to be under grace today, does not exclude laws.

So then, what exactly does it mean to be under law vs. under grace? It probably means to be under the authority of one of 2 covenants...

- The covenant from ~1445 B.C. - 30 A.D. vs. the covenant from ~30 A.D. - the end

- The covenant characterized by sin vs. the covenant characterized by obedience
- The law covenant vs. the grace covenant
- The Old Covenant vs. the New Covenant

Why then, is the Old Covenant called "law," and the New Covenant called "grace?" Here is the likely reason...

Old Covenant "sanctification" blessings were based on law (works), while New Covenant blessings are based on promise (grace).

19. "But Love Is the Only Law"

It's hard to believe that anyone can read the hundreds of commands in the New Testament and conclude there's only one command: Love. Yet, some hold that view based on the following verses...

> "Owe no one anything, except to love each other, for the one who loves another has fulfilled the law. The commandments, 'You shall not commit adultery, You shall not murder, You shall not steal, You shall not covet,' and *any other commandment, are summed up in this word:* 'You shall love your neighbor as yourself.' Love does no wrong to a neighbor; therefore *love is the fulfilling of the law"* (Rom. 13:8-10).

> *"For the whole law is fulfilled in one word:* 'You shall love your neighbor as yourself." (Gal. 5:14).

Thomas Schreiner comments on Romans 13:8-10,

> "The first mistake is to say that since love fulfills the law we no longer have any need for commandments. Some understand these verses to say that the only moral guideline Christians need is love...Those who believe this way bristle against imposing any commands upon believers. They think this is a form of legalism. They condemn as legalism any commands which say 'you should do this,' or 'you should not do this.' They insist that believers are not under any 'commands,' except the command to love one another."[24]

Love is only the motivation, not the definition, for our obedience. Love merely summarizes those commands from the law. What does love motivate us to do specifically?

Suppose a man says, "I love my neighbor's wife." How do we know that's not love? Because Jesus defines how to love in His teaching and commands, "Everyone who divorces his wife and marries another commits adultery..." (Lk. 16:18)

---

[24] Thomas R. Schreiner, "Sermon: Loving One Another Fulfills the Law: Romans 13:8-10," in *Southern Baptist Journal of Theology,* 2007:11, 104-109.

Plus, love can't be the only law because the New Testament speaks positively of Christ's plural commandments...

"If you love Me, you will keep My *commandmentS*" (Jn. 14:15).

"Whoever has My *commandmentS* and keeps them, he it is who loves me..." (Jn. 14:21).

"If you keep My *commandmentS,* you will abide in My love..." (Jn. 15:10).

"For neither circumcision counts for anything, nor uncircumcision, but keeping the *commandmentS* of God" (1 Cor. 7:19).

"For you know what *instructionS* we gave you through the Lord Jesus" (1 Thes. 4:2).

"And by this we know that we have come to know Him, if we keep His *commandments*" (1 Jn. 2:3).

"and whatever we ask we receive from Him, because we keep His *commandmentS* and do what pleases him" (1 Jn. 3:22).

"Whoever keeps His *commandmentS* abides in Him, and He in them..." (1 Jn. 3:24).

"By this we know that we love the children of God, when we love God and obey his *commandmentS*. For this is the love of God, that we keep his *commandmentS*. And his *commandmentS* are not burdensome" (1 Jn. 5:2-3).

"And this is love, that we walk according to his *commandmentS...* " (2 Jn. 6).

"...her offspring, on those who keep the *commandmentS* of God..." (Rev. 12:17).

Clearly, our Lord gave us hundreds of commands, not just one to obey. Those commands define how to love. And, our love for Him motivates us to obey His commands.

Two similar errors emphasize the new heart or the indwelling Spirit at the expense of Christ's commands. But again, they merely beg the question, "What do regeneration and the indwelling Spirit motivate us to do?" Trust in Christ and obey His commands. Regeneration and the Spirit merely motivate, but don't define our obedience.

All 3 truths (the new heart, indwelling Spirit, and God's commands) are combined in Ezekiel 36:26-27.

> "And I will give you a *new heart,* and a *new Spirit* I will put within you. And I will remove the heart of stone from your flesh and give you a *heart of flesh.* And I will *put my Spirit within you,* and cause you to *walk in my statutes and be careful to obey my rules."*

Imagine a man who claims that his regenerate heart or the indwelling Spirit told him to love his neighbor's wife. How do we know the Spirit didn't tell him that? Because Christ's teaching and commands define love as being faithful to your spouse by avoiding adultery.

Beware of false dichotomies between the Spirit and the law of Christ. The New Testament contrasts between the Spirit and the law refer to the law of Moses for the unregenerate, not the law of Christ for the regenerate (cf. Rom. 7:6; 2 Cor. 3:6; Gal. 5:18). The Spirit and Christ's law are a both-and, not an either-or. Remember, the Holy Spirit is the One Who inspired all those hundreds of commands in the New Testament.

20. "But the New Covenant Law Is Written in the Heart, Not the New Testament"

Since the New Covenant law is written in the heart (Heb. 8:10), does that mean that it's not also written in the New Testament?

Let's explore what the words "write on the heart" mean by surveying parallel verses. We find the idea of "writing on the heart" at least 6 times in Scripture...

"Write My Laws on the Heart" and "Bind Them on the Body" Means "Keep My Commands"

1. "My son, do not forget my teaching, but let your heart *keep my commandments,* for length of days and years of life and peace they will add to you. Let not steadfast love and faithfulness *forsake you; bind them around your neck; write them on the tablet of your heart"* (Pr. 3:1-3).

2. "My son, *keep my words and treasure up my commandments* with you; *keep my commandments* and live; *keep my teaching* as the apple of your eye; *bind them on your fingers; write them on the tablet of your heart"* (Pr. 7:1-3).

Sin (Disobedience to God's Law) Can Be Written on the Heart

3. "The sin of Judah is written with a pen of iron, with a point of diamond it is *engraved on the tablet of their heart,* and on the horns of their altars, while their children remember their altars and their Asherim" (Jer. 17:1-2).

"Put My Laws in Their Hearts/Minds" Results in Obedience

4. *"I will put my law within them, and I will write it on their hearts.* And I will be their God, and they shall be my people" (Jer. 31:33; cf. Heb. 8:10).

"Written on Our Heart" Likely Means "Loved by Us"

6. "You yourselves are our letter of recommendation, *written on our hearts (loved by us),* to be known and read by all. And

you show that you are a letter from Christ delivered by us, written not with ink but with the Spirit of the living God, not on tablets of stone but on tablets of human hearts" (2 Cor. 3:2-3).

In addition to those 6 passages, there are at least 3 similar passages about *binding* God's commands on the heart and body. This is significant because in Pr. 3:3 and 7:3 above, "write commands on the tablet of your heart" = "bind them around your neck/ fingers" = "keep My commands." So, writing on the heart, binding on the body, and obeying are likely synonyms from Hebrew parallelism.

Binding God's Commands on the Heart/Body
Is a Metaphor for Obeying His Commands

"My son, *keep your father's commandment, and forsake not your mother's teaching. Bind them on your heart always; tie them around your neck"* (Pr. 6:20-21; cf. 1:9).

"You shall love the Lord your God with all your heart and with all your soul and with all your might. *And these words that I command you today shall be on your heart...You shall bind them as a sign on your hand..."* (Deut. 6:4-8).

"And if you will indeed *obey my commandments...*You shall therefore *lay up these words of mine in your heart and in your soul, and you shall bind them as a sign on your hand, and they shall be as frontlets between your eyes. You shall teach them* to your children..." (Deut. 11:13, 18-19).

The Old Covenant Law
Was In Regenerate Saints' Hearts and the Old Testament

"And these words that I command you today shall be on your heart" (Deut. 6:6).

"You shall therefore *lay up these words of mine in your heart and in your soul..."* (Deut. 11:18).

"I desire to do your will, O my God; *your law is within my heart"* (Ps. 40:8).

"I have stored up your word in my heart, that I might not sin against you" (Ps. 119:11).

Antinomianism errs by reading the word "only" into Heb. 8:10, like this, "I will put my laws into their minds, and write them (ONLY) on their hearts (not in the New Testament)..."

Remember earlier, we saw that Old Covenant saints probably already had all 7 New Covenant blessings from Jer. 31:31-34, including the law written both in their hearts and the Old Testament. So, New Covenant saints can also have the New Covenant law of Christ written both in their hearts and the New Testament.

In Hebrew and Greek, the heart is the center of the mind, emotions, will, desires, etc. So, God writing His New Covenant law in our hearts is a metaphor meaning He will regenerate our hearts to remember, love, and obey His laws.

Plus, since the law in the heart is a metaphor, we need to be careful about trying to reason additional doctrine from it. The hermeneutics of metaphor will not allow us to reason, "Since God's law is written in the heart, therefore it is not written in the New Testament."

Metaphors communicate that A is like B in some ways, but not all ways. So, beware of pressing a metaphor's details since it's designed to illustrate only some truths. Metaphors, parables, and types are all designed to symbolize major themes, not details.

In conclusion, God writing His laws on our hearts has nothing to do with content or location, that is, the heart instead of the New Testament. "...God's love has been poured into our hearts..." (Rom. 5:5) does not mean that His love is not also recorded in Scripture. He wrote His law in the New Testament, and made it precious to our regenerate hearts, guaranteeing our obedience.

Part IV.
4 Reasons Why
All New Testament Laws Are for Our Obedience

Moses' Law Prepared Unjustified, Spirit-Less Slaves
For Christ's 1st Coming

One reason why God gave the law of Moses to Israel was to tutor/ prepare them for Messiah's 1st coming, so they might be justified by faith, adopted, and Spirit indwelled. But now, we don't need the Mosaic law to tutor/prepare us because Messiah has already come, we are justified by faith (Gal. 3:23-25), adopted (Gal. 3:26 - 4:7), and Spirit-indwelled (Gal. 5:18).

Christ's Law Helps Prepare Justified, Spirit-Indwelled Heirs
For His 2nd Coming

Moses' law prepared unjustified, Spirit-less slaves for Christ's 1st coming. But, Christ's law helps prepare justified, Spirit-indwelled heirs for His 2nd coming.

21. The Apostles Gave Hundreds of Commands After the Cross

The 4 gospels, Acts, and the epistles give us hundreds of commands. These letters were written from ~45 - 95 A.D., decades after Christ's death in ~30 A.D. So, if all laws and commands passed away when Christ died, then why did the apostles still give us more commands later? Obviously, for us to obey...

"...He had given *commands* through the Holy Spirit to the apostles whom He had chosen" (Acts. 1:2).

"teaching them to *observe all that I have commanded* you..." (Mt. 28:20).

"...*what instructions we gave you* through the Lord Jesus" (1 Thes. 4:2).

22. Sin Is Lawlessness

How could God still call sinners "lawless" unless He still has a law? The lawless violate God's law of conscience. Sin is "commandlessness." Practicing sin = practicing no law.

Sin Is Lawlessness:
"Everyone who makes a practice of sinning also practices lawlessness; *sin is lawlessness"* (1 Jn. 3:4).

The Lawless Will Not Enter the Kingdom of Heaven:
"Not everyone who says to me, 'Lord, Lord,' will enter the kingdom of heaven...I never knew you; depart from me, you workers of *lawlessness"* (Mt. 7:21, 23).

Antichrist Is Lawless:
"...the man of *lawlessness* is revealed..." (2 Th. 2:3, cf. 2:8-9)

The New Covenant Has Laws:
"...I will establish a new covenant...I will put *my laws* into their minds, and write them on their hearts..." (Heb. 8:8, 10; cf. Is. 42:1, 4; Ezek. 11:19-20, 36:26-27; 1 Cor. 9:21; Gal. 6:2).

Yes, God still has a law today for Christians to obey. And, that law is the law of Christ in the New Testament.

23. The Bible Never Criticizes the Law of Christ, But Praises It

Some Covenant Theologians think that the law of Christ = the law of Moses. However, does the law of Christ include, "...nor shall you wear a garment of cloth made of two kinds of material?" (Lev. 19:19). And, does the Law of Moses include, "Make disciples of all nations, baptizing them...?" (Mt. 28:19). No, the law of Moses and the law of Christ obviously refer to 2 different time periods in redemptive history.

The Bible criticizes the law of Moses, but never the law of Christ. In fact, the Bible praises the law of Christ...

Christ Is a New Lawgiver, Not Just a Law Keeper:
See the "12 New Commands From Christ's New Law" below.

Messiah's Law Is for the Gentiles:
"...He will bring forth justice to the nations...the coastlands shall wait for *His law*" (Is. 42:1, 4).

Christians Are Not Lawless, But In-Lawed to Christ:
"...not being without law of God, but *in-lawed (Gk.) to Christ...*" (1 Cor. 9:21).

We Must Fulfill the Law of Christ:
"Bear one another's burdens, and so *fulfill the law of Christ*" (Gal. 6:2).

What exactly is the law of Christ? Scripture doesn't tell us. But, it may be all laws given by Christ and His apostles in the New Testament. Doug Moo thinks that in addition to those laws it includes the Holy Spirit's enablement and the motivation of love...

"It is more difficult to determine whether the law of Christ includes specific teachings and principles. Many deny that this is the case, but their reasons for doing so often betray a bias against finding any specific demands as binding on Christians. The work of Schrage and others has shown that Paul and the other apostles were quite willing to impose specific commandments on their charges; and these commandments were, in fact, often drawn from, or reflective of, Jesus' own teachings. For these reasons, I think it is highly probable that Paul thought of the law of Christ as including within it the teachings of Jesus and the apostolic witness, based on his life and teaching, about what it means to reverence God in daily life. This is not, however, to deny the importance of love or the direction of the Spirit. The 'law of Christ,' Paul's shorthand expression for that form of God's law applicable to new covenant believers, includes all these. Longenecker's succinct summary says it well: The law of Christ stands in Paul's thought for those 'prescriptive principles stemming from the heart of the gospel (usually embodied in the example and teachings of Jesus), which are meant to be applied to specific situations by the direction and enablement of the Holy Spirit, being always motivated and conditioned by love.'"[25]

Moo may be right. But, it's not important whether the phrase "law of Christ" includes Christ's laws alone, or also the Holy Sprit and love, since we agree they're included in the New Testament, and crucial for obedience. Remember, this book focuses on which laws to obey (N.T.), more than how to obey (the Holy Spirit's grace) and why to obey (love). Even as the law of Moses functioned as both regulation and revelation, so may the law of Christ.

---

[25] Moo, in Gundry, 369.

24. Jesus Christ Is Lord

Jesus Christ is Lord (Master). Who ever heard of a Master who didn't give any orders to his servants? And, who ever heard of servants with no duties?

Jesus Christ is Prophet, Priest, and King. As the new Prophet, He gave new teachings. As the new Priest, He made a new sacrifice. And, as the new King, he gave a new law. Every King has a law.

To sum it all up, Jesus Christ is the new Lawgiver of the New Covenant in the New Testament canon. He and His apostles transferred some old commands, and gave us dozens of new commands...

12, New Commands From Christ's New Law

Jesus Christ is the new Lawgiver who instituted a New Covenant, containing new commands, surrounded by a new body of canon literature. Here are 12, new types of commands...

1. New Commands for New Covenant Symbols:

> *"Go...baptizing them* in the name of the Father and of the Son and of the Holy Spirit" (Mt. 28:19).

> "...This is My body, which is given for you. *Do this in remembrance of Me"* (Lk. 22:19).

2. New Commands for New Covenant Blessing:

> "...but *be filled with the Spirit"* (Eph. 5:18).

Under the Old Covenant, the Holy Spirit temporarily indwelt some leaders of the covenant people. Under the New Covenant, He permanently indwells all of the covenant people.

Citing examples of the Spirit indwelling some Old Testament saints at some times does not prove that He indwelled all saints always. (That would be like claiming that since Enoch was raptured, therefore all Old Testament saints were raptured.) Such examples only prove that He indwelt those particular ones at those particular times.

In such questions it is helpful to remember the 2 hermeneutics narration vs. declaration, and description vs. prescription. The Old Testament examples of Spirit indwelling are *narrations* of what happened to some leaders, not *declarations* of what happened to all saints.

In the New Testament we have declarations about the Spirit's indwelling (1 Cor. 6:19, Gal. 4:6) and a prescription about the Spirit's filling (Eph. 5:18) making these blessings normative for all New Covenant Christians at all times.

3. <u>New Commands for New Religious Leaders</u>:

> *"Therefore an overseer must be..."* (1 Tim. 3:2).
>
> *"Deacons likewise must be..."* (1 Tim. 3:8).
>
> *"...appoint elders* in every city..." (Tit. 1:5).

4. <u>New Command for a New Government System</u>:

> "Let every person *be subject to the governing authorities"* (Rom. 13:1).
>
> *"Be subject* for the Lord's sake to every human institution, whether it be *to the emperor* as supreme, or to governors..." (1 Pet. 2:13-14).

The Old Covenant commanded obedience to Israel, a state-church theocracy. The New Covenant commands obedience to the state government.

5. <u>New Commands for a New Judicial System</u>:

> "But if he does not listen, *take one or two others along with you...*If he refuses to hear them, *tell it to the church.* And if he refuses to listen even to the church, *let him be to you as a Gentile and a tax-collector"* (Mt. 18:16-17).

"When one of you has a grievance against another, does he dare go to law before the unrighteous instead of the saints?... So if you have such cases, why do you lay them before those who have no standing in the church?" (1 Cor. 6:1, 4).

6. New Command for a New Revenue System:

"...Is it lawful to pay taxes to Caesar or not?...*render to Caesar the things that are Caesar's..."* (Mt. 22:17, 21).

"Pay to all what is owed to them: taxes to whom taxes are owed..." (Rom. 13:7).

Both covenants commanded the paying of taxes, but to different authorities. The Old Covenant commanded paying taxes to the theocracy of Israel, thus to Jehovah. But, the New Covenant commands paying taxes to the state, thus to Caesar.

7. New Command for a New Welfare System:

"If any believing woman has relatives who are widows, let her care for them. Let the church not be burdened, so *that it may care for those who are really widows"* (1 Tim. 5:16).

8. New Command for a New Educational System:

"Go therefore and make disciples of all nations... teaching them to observe all that I have commanded you..." (Mt. 28:19-20).

Deuteronomy 6:6-7 commanded proselytizing of Jewish children, but the New Covenant commands the proselytizing of all Gentiles. (In the Old Testament, God also commanded the evangelism of some, but not all, Gentiles like the Ninevites.)

9. New Commands for Marriage:

"But I say to you that everyone who divorces *his wife, except on the ground of sexual immorality..."* (Mt. 5:32, cf. Deut. 21:13-14, 24:1-4; Lev. 20:10).

The Old Covenant law allowed divorce for any reason. (Divorce was not a "crime," but it was still a sin. cf. Mt. 19:4-9) But under the New Covenant, divorce is allowed only for abandonment or sexual immorality. Laws for an unregenerate nation were more tolerant than laws for a regenerate Church.

> "...But if her husband dies, she is free to be *married to whom she wishes, only in the Lord"* (1 Cor. 7:39).

Under the Old Covenant, Jews could marry only other Jews (Ex. 34:16; Deut. 7:3; Ezra 10:2; Neh. 13:23-27) even an unregenerate spouse. But under the New Covenant, Christians can marry from any Gentile nation, but only a regenerate spouse.

> "Therefore an overseer must be...*the husband of one wife...*" (1 Tim. 3:2; Tit. 1:5-6).

The Old Covenant allowed polygamy (Ex. 21:10-11) for all men, including leaders. The New Covenant commands monogamy for church leaders.

10. New Commands for Prayers:

> "Let us then *with confidence draw near to the throne of grace...*" (Heb. 4:16, cf. 10:19-22)

The Old Covenant restricted access to God's visible presence to one man (the High Priest) once a year (on the day of Atonement). The New Covenant allows all saints to access the throne of grace always.

> "...I urge that supplications, *prayers,* intercessions, and thanksgivings be made for all people, *for kings* and all who are in high positions..." (1 Tim. 2:1-2).

The New Covenant commands prayers for Gentile rulers.

> "...whatever you *ask of the Father in My name* He will give it to you. Until now you have asked nothing in My name..." (Jn. 16:23-24).

11. <u>New Commands for Example and Motivation</u>:

> "A new commandment I give to you, that you love one another: *Just as I have loved you, you also are to love one another"* (Jn.. 13:34).

The Old Covenant command "Love your neighbor as yourself" required a self-like love toward others. Christ transferred that command into His New Covenant.

In addition to that command, He gave a new and higher command to love our brothers with a love patterned after His self-sacrificial love. This command required not just a self-like love, but a self-denying love. He commanded us to selflessly love only our Christian brothers, not all the people of the world. The example, motivation, and object of our love are new.

> "Now *as the church submits to Christ,* so also wives should submit in everything to their husbands" (Eph. 5:24).

> "Husbands, *love your wives, as Christ also loved the church and gave Himself up for her"* (Eph. 5:25).

12. <u>New Commands for New Covenant Canon Revelation</u>:

> "And when this letter has been read among you, *have it also read in the church of the Laodiceans;* and see that you also *read the letter from Laodicea"* (Col. 4:16).

> "I put you under oath before the Lord to have *this letter read* to all the brothers" (1 Thes. 5:27).

Part V.
Conclusion:
Sanctification Is Christ-Centered, Not Law-Centered

In conclusion, we can summarize the application of God's law to us with these 5 facts…

1. The whole Old Testament is still useful for faith/doctrine.
2. All Old Testament commands were cancelled.
3. Some of those O.T. commands were transferred to the N.T.
4. All New Testament commands are for our obedience.
5. Our obedience is often motivated by Christ's example (see below).

All practices based on the Old Covenant, law of Moses have ceased, including:

- The priesthood and sacrifices (Roman Catholicism, etc.)
- State-Church theocracy (Roman Catholicism, and dominion/ reconstructionism/theonomy of historic, Covenant Theology)

- Infant baptism (Roman Catholicism, Covenant Theology, etc.)
- Dietary laws (Adventism, etc.)
- Sabbath-keeping (Adventism, Covenant Theology, etc.)

Once you understand that all Old Covenant practices are cancelled, that undermines the foundation of all Old Covenant-based groups including Romanism, Mormonism, Adventism, and Covenantalism (Covenant Theology).

> **"Once you understand that all Old Covenant practices are cancelled, that undermines the foundation of all Old Covenant-based groups including Romanism, Mormonism, Adventism, and Covenantalism..."**

Jon Zens observed 3 popular views of the Old Testament's main theme...

1. "Law-centered" (some Covenant Theologians).
2. "Israel-centered" (some Dispensationalists).
3. "Christ-centered"[26] (New Covenant Theology).

The Old Testament's hero isn't the Torah itself, rather it's the promised Messiah Himself...

> "You search *the Scriptures* because you think that in them you have eternal life; and it is they that *bear witness about Me*...If you believed Moses, you would believe Me; *for he wrote of Me*" (Jn. 5:39, 46).

> "and beginning with Moses and all the Prophets, He interpreted to them in all the Scriptures *the things concerning Himself... everything written about Me in the Law of Moses and the Prophets and the Psalms* must be fulfilled. Then He opened their minds to understand the Scriptures, and said to them, Thus it is written, that the Christ should suffer and on the third day rise from the dead, and that repentance and forgiveness of

---

[26] Jon Zens, "This Is My Beloved Son, Hear Him: The Foundation for New Covenant Ethics and Ecclesiology" in *Searching Together*, 1997, 23:2-4.

sins should be proclaimed in His name to all nations..." (Lk. 24:17, 44-47).

Well, hopefully now you can harmonize all the positive and negative verses about the Law. And, hopefully you have a better idea of how to "...be holy, for I am holy" (1 Pet. 1:16).

We have not come to Mt. Sinai with its fire and smoke, darkness and lightning. But, we have come to Mt. Zion and Jesus the Mediator of the New Covenant. We are citizens of the Jerusalem above, not the earthly Jerusalem (Heb. 12:18-24).

If you've come unto Christ, He's given you rest from your works. Remember Him Who says, "All authority in heaven and on earth has been given to Me...Therefore...obey all that I have commanded" (Mt. 28:20).

Doctrinal Truths About Christ Often Motivate Our Obedience

Remember at the beginning of this study, I said we would focus more on which commands to obey, than why to obey? Well, now it's time to think briefly about why we obey (motives to obedience).

The ultimate motive for our obedience is probably love for God. The greatest command is "Love the Lord your God with all your heart..." And, "If you love Me, you will keep My commandments" (Jn. 14:15).

Plus, the Lord uses numerous other motives to help us obey, such as His attributes, His great works in redemptive history, promises, thankfulness, warnings, doctrinal truths about Christ, etc. (By the way, that's why "those who learn little doctrine, grow little.")

If you want to mature in Christ, look unto Jesus. The Lord often motivates us to obey by a command (imperative) in the context of a doctrinal truth (indicative.) Duty-centered preachers burden their hearers. But, Christ-centered preachers know how to edify and motivate their listeners to obedience by teaching doctrine-inspired duty.

That's why in Romans, Paul spent chapters 1-11 explaining mostly doctrine, before giving mostly commands in 12-16. And in Ephesians, he explained mostly doctrine in chapters 1-3, followed by mostly practical application in 4-6.

The reasons why we obey include the examples of Christ's birth, life, death, resurrection, mediation, and return (not memorizing the Decalogue).

<u>Christ's Birth Motivates Us to Humility</u>:
"Have this mind among yourselves, which is yours in Christ Jesus, who, though He was in the form of God, did not count equality with God a thing to be held onto, but made Himself nothing, taking the form of a servant, being born in the likeness of men" (Phil. 2:5-7; 2 Cor. 8:7-9).

<u>Christ's Life Motivates Us to Holy Living</u>:
"...whoever says he abides in Him ought to *walk in the same way in which He walked"* (1 Jn. 2:6; Mt. 20:27-28; Jn. 13:15; 1 Pet. 2:21-23).

<u>Christ's Death Motivates Us to Love One Another</u>:
"A new commandment I give to you, that you love one another; just *as I have loved you,* you also are to love one another...Greater love has no one than this, that someone lays down his life for his friends" (Jn. 13:34, 15:12-13; Rom. 6:2-13; 1 Cor. 6:20; 2 Cor. 5:14-15; Gal. 2:20; Eph. 5:2, 5:25-27; Col. 2:20-23; Tit. 2:14; Heb. 12:1-3; 1 Jn. 3:16, 4:10-11).

<u>Christ's Resurrection Motivates Us to Live the New Life</u>:
"...just as Christ was raised from the dead by the glory of the Father, we too might walk in newness of life" (Rom. 6:4ff.; Col. 3:1-2).

<u>Christ's Mediation Motivates Us to Hold Fast Our Confession</u>:
"Since then we have a great high priest who has passed through the heavens, Jesus, the Son of God, let us hold fast our confession. For we do not have a high priest who is unable to sympathize with our weaknesses..." (Heb. 4:14-16, 10:19-22).

Christ's Return Motivates Us to Purity:
"…when He appears we shall be like Him, because we shall see
Him as He is. And everyone who thus hopes in him *purifies
himself* as He is pure" (1 Jn. 3:2-3; Mt. 24:42-44; Rom. 14:10-13,
15:1-3; 1 Cor. 15:58; 2 Cor. 5:9-11; Col. 3:4-5; 1 Thes. 4:18, 5:6; 2
Pet. 3:11-14; 1 Jn. 2:28).

Can you see, it's all about Christ, not Moses? If you want to grow
in grace, Christ will sanctify you far more than Moses ever could.
Study Him to grow like Him.

Here is a chart summarizing many of the conclusions in this
book…

3 Different Views of the Law of God Throughout Redemptive History			
Issue in Question?	**Reformed, Covenant Theology**	**New Covenant Theology**	**Anti-nomianism**
What is the main hermeneutic?	The unity of the covenants, because there is one covenant of grace.	Progressive revelation (The N.T. interprets the O.T. The apostles' herm., the N.T. herm., the N.C. herm.)	? (Grace and law can't co-exist during the same time.)
What is the eternal, unchanging law of God for all people, of all times?	The Ten Command-ments.	The sins lists for all humans, including the Gentiles.	There is no law period, because we're not under law, but under grace.
Can the Old Covenant, law of Moses be divided, into 3 parts?	Yes, 3 parts: Moral, civil, & ceremonial.	No.	No.

What is the relation between the Old Covenant & the New Covenant?	The N.C. is a newer administration of the O.C., since they're both different administrations of the one covenant of grace.	Type & Antitype: The O.C. was the type, and the N.C. is the antitype.	?
How many Old Testament commands were cancelled?	Those commands not specifically cancelled in the N.T. are still in force. 2 major views: 1. Non-theonomic: The civil & ceremonial laws were cancelled, but the Pre-Sinai & moral laws still abide. 2. Theonomy/ Dominion/ Reconstruction: The ceremonial laws were cancelled, but the Pre-Sinai, moral, & civil laws still abide.	All.	All.

How do we use the Old Testament?	Faith + obedience.	Faith (teaching, rebuke, correction, training in righteousness, example, warning, evangelism, & history) but not direct obedience.	?
What is the relation between Old Testament commands quoted in the New Testament	Continuation.	Transferred.	We're not under any law (O.T. or N.T.) but under grace.
Can a Christian break the Ten Command- ments?	A Christian who stole, violated both Eph. 4:28 and Ex. 20:15.	A Christian who stole violated Eph. 4:28, not Ex. 20:15.	A Christian who stole did not violate Ex. 20:15 or Eph. 4:28 since we are not under law, but under grace.
Which New Testament commands must we obey?	All.	All.	None, since we're not under law, but under grace. (Some claim there is only one command: Love.)

What does it mean to be not under law, but under grace?	We're not under the ceremonial (& maybe the civil) law, but under grace.	We're not under the law covenant (O.C.) but under the grace covenant (N.C.) Just as there was grace given during the time of the old, law covenant, so there is law given during the time of the new, grace covenant.	We're not under any laws (defined rules), but under grace.
What is the law of Christ?	? (The law of Christ is not clearly distinguished from the law of Moses.)	The law of Christ is all commands and teaching by Christ & His apostles, located in the N.T. (the N.C. canon).	? (The law of Christ is not clearly distinguished from the law of Moses.)

Appendix I:
Does New Covenant Theology
Allow Beastiality and Incest?

One of the hottest arguments against New Covenant Theology in blogs and forums goes something like this:

"Since the New Testament doesn't state that beastiality and incest are sins, therefore New Covenant Theology can't be true." (Just try to follow the "logic" behind that one!)

That argument was probably popularized by Greg Bahnsen, the famous theonomist, Covenant Theologian. And, Covenant Theologians often hurl that argument against New Covenant Theology.

However, the same type of argument could easily be made against the Old Testament. Where does the Old Testament *explicitly* state that the following are sins:

1. Abortion?

2. Porn?
3. Pedophilia?
4. Being a pimp?
5. Oral sex before marriage?
6. Buying an idol?
7. Trying to buy the power of the Holy Spirit? (Acts 8:20)
8. Lovers of themselves? (2 Tim. 3:2)
9. Lovers of money? (2 Tim. 3:2)
10. Etc.

And, if you put your mind to it, I'm sure you could think of many more examples of so-called "moral sins" that aren't stated explicitly in the Old Testament.

Two Assumptions: Explicit and Exhaustive

The problem with the beastiality/incest objection is that it depends on 2 unexamined assumptions:

1. The Old Covenant contains an explicit and exhaustive revelation of "moral law."

2. The New Testament must contain an explicit and exhaustive revelation of "moral law."

However, neither the Old Testament nor the New Testament explicitly reveal ALL the laws of conscience. (If they did, the Bible would have to be the size of *Webster's Unabridged Dictionary*!) We know some things are wrong because "we know that we know" (conscience).

Even though the objections about beastiality and incest are irrelevant to New Covenant Theology because of the 2 assumptions above, let's discuss them anyway.

All Christians agree that humans have consciences convicting them of certain "sins." But, God never explicitly defines those sins for us in Scripture. However, He does tell us in certain sin lists the standards by which He will judge all men for heaven or hell.

I believe that the sin lists for all humans (including Gentiles) are the most likely definition of the "law of conscience" (Rom. 1:18-32; 1 Cor. 6:9-10; Gal. 5:19-21; Rev. 21:8, 22:15). Notice that beastiality (Lev. 18:23) and incest (Lev. 18:6-17) are part of a list of the sins of the Gentiles (Lev. 18:3, 18:24-30).

Even though the whole law of Moses (including Lev. 18) was cancelled as Old Covenant (but not Old Testament), the same sins in Lev. 18 may also be recorded in Gentiles' consciences. So, if a heathen living in a rainforest commits incest today, he violates the law of conscience, not Lev. 18:9.

Were beastiality and incest sins before Moses wrote Lev. 18 in the 15th century B.C.? Then, they were still sins after God cancelled Lev. 18 in ~30 A.D. They were part of God's conscience law which transcends His covenants' laws. (Although, incest may not have been revealed as a sin to the conscience until after Adam and Eve's early descendants had children.)

Majoring on the Minors

Questions about beastiality, incest, etc. are peripheral to New Covenant Theology because of the 2 assumptions above. Such questions major on the minors. They're really rabbit trails diverting from the main issues:

1. Are Jer. 31:31-33; Mt. 5:17-18; Rom. 3:31; and 2 Tim. 3:16-17 really proof texts for Covenant Theology against New Covenant Theology? (Or, are some of them actually proof texts for New Covenant Theology against Covenant Theology?)

2. Does the Bible teach one Covenant of Grace, or 2 major covenants (structured by one purpose of grace)?

3. How can the law of Moses be divided into 3 parts when it's one whole unit? (Gal. 3:10, 5:3; Jas. 2:10).

4. How can the whole Decalogue still be binding when God calls it "the covenant" (which was cancelled)?

5. How can the Sabbath be changed to the first day of the week when the first day is called "one/first (day) from the Sabbath," in the Greek?

In conclusion, New Covenant Theology doesn't allow beastiality and incest any more than the Old Covenant allowed abortion and porn.

Appendix II:
13 Ways How We Still Use the Whole Old Testament

Trying to read the New Testament without the Old Testament is like trying to watch a movie after missing the first half. You can't understand the plot.

The Bible is a story. God chose to reveal Himself to us in a story. And, the Old Testament is the foundation to understanding the whole story.

In short, we use the Old Testament for faith, but not direct obedience. Lorraine Boettner said it well,

"The Old Testament is our history book, not our law book."[27]

In the early church, Marcionism was an error that discarded the Old Testament for both faith and obedience. Some critics have

---

[27] Loraine Boettner, "Response to Dispensational Premillennialism," in *The Meaning of the Millennium*, Robert G. Clouse, Ed., (Downers Grove: IVP, 1977), 98.

tried to label New Covenant Theology as Marcionism. However, if Covenant Theology's view that 1/3-2/3 of the Old Testament law is cancelled isn't Marcionism, then New Covenant Theology's view that 3/3 of the Old Testament law is cancelled isn't Marcionism.

> "Jesus is no Marcionite; and even if his followers are no longer bound by the commandments of the law, they are still to read and profit from it."[28]

The following verses show that we still use the whole Old Testament today for teaching/faith (everything but obedience).

1-4. Instruction, Endurance, Encouragement, and Hope:
"For whatever was written in former days was written for our *instruction,* that through *endurance* and through the *encouragement* of the Scriptures we might have *hope"* (Rom. 15:4).

5-6. Example, and Avoiding Temptation and Sin:
"Now these things took place as *examples* for us, that we might *not desire evil* as they did...Now these things happened to them as an *example,* but they were written down for our *instruction... "* (1 Cor. 10:6, 11; cf. Mt. 4:4, 4:7, 4:10).

7-11. Salvation, Teaching, Reproof, Correction, and Righteousness:
"and how from childhood you have been acquainted with the sacred writings, which are able to make you *wise for salvation* through faith in Christ Jesus. All Scripture is breathed out by God and profitable *for teaching, for reproof, for correction, and for training in righteousness"* (2 Tim. 3:15-16).

12. Evangelism With the Gospel of Messiah:
"...reasoned from the Scriptures, explaining and proving that it was necessary for the Christ to suffer and to rise from the dead..." (Acts 17:2-3, cf. 2:21, 2:25-28, 2:34-35, 8:32-35, 13:32-41, 18:28; Rom. 4:23-25).

---

[28] Moo, in Gundry, 353.

13. Understand Fulfillment of Prophecy:
"...everything written about me in the Law of Moses and the
Prophets and the Psalms must be fulfilled" (Lk. 24:44, cf. 4:21,
18:31, 21:22; Mt. 2:15, 2:17, 2:23, 5:17-18, 13:14, 13:35, 26:56,
27:9; Jn. 17:12, 18:32, 19:24, 19:28, 19:36; Acts 1:16, 3:18,
13:33).

Following Jesus in the New Covenant

Thank you for taking the time to read this book. Has the Lord
taught you anything? What's in your mind now: A bright light bulb
or a dark cloud?

Why not pray right now, "Lord, what do you want me to believe?
And, what do you want me to do? Help me to follow You Jesus,
wherever You lead, whatever the cost."

What do you think of *ALL Old Testament Laws Cancelled*? Do you
want to tell your friends about it? If so, consider sharing your
review (whether pro or con) at Amazon, Facebook, MySpace, etc.

To order more copies of this book, visit JesusSaidFollowMe.org

Annotated Bibliography of the Most Helpful Sources

Roger Fellows, *The Law and the Christian*, Sovereign Grace
Fellowship, sgfcanada.com/?page_id=10

Clear-thinking on the law of God throughout redemptive history.
His main points include...

1. All people are at all times subject to God's laws.

2. Sin is defined in terms of law.

3. We must not equate God's unchanging laws with the law of
Moses.

4. The whole Mosaic law is abrogated or cancelled under the new
covenant.

5. This does not leave the believer without law.

6. God's moral requirements for people don't change substantially.

Summary: "The Mosaic law was given to Israel in the form of a covenant, the essence of which was the Ten Commandments. This law has been abrogated by Christ. Believers today are not under Moses' law, but under Christ's law. This entails obedience to all the commands given under the new covenant, although much of that which is binding on Christians is the same as that which was binding on Israel..."

Stanley N. Gundry, Editor, *Five Views on Law and Gospel,* (Grand Rapids: Zondervan, 1999).

This book is a debate on the law between 5 different authors...

   1. Covenant Theology by Willem Vangemeren
   2. Theonomic, Covenant Theology by Greg Bahnsen
   3. Decalogue = Moral Law (similar to C.T.) by Walter Kaiser
   4. Dispensationalism by Wayne Strickland
   5. Modified Lutheran View (similar to N.C.T.) by Doug Moo.

Meredith Kline, *The Structure of Biblical Authority*, Revised edition, (Grand Rapids: Eerdmans, 1975).

Kline took archaeology discoveries from ancient, near east treaties and applied them to law, canon, and Scripture. God designed the Old Covenant with several similarities to these treaties.

In summary, 2 covenants requires 2 canons, the Old Covenant canon (Old Testament) and the New Covenant canon (New Testament). Two covenants = 2 canon rules, in one Bible.

John Reisinger, *Abraham's Four Seeds*, (Frederick, MD: New Covenant Media, 1998). "An examination of the basic presuppositions of Covenant Theology and Dispensationalism as they each relate to the promise of God to 'Abraham and his seed.'"

This is a challenging book to infant baptism. Esau and Ishmael were so-called "covenant children." It distinguishes 4 seeds of Abraham:

1. Physical Jews (Gen. 21:13)
2. Nation of Israel (Ex. 19:6)
3. Church (Gal. 3:7-9)
4. Christ (Gal. 3:16)

This book would have been even clearer if it distinguished only 2 seeds and their offspring:

1. Abraham's Physical Seed: Ethnic Jews and their offspring (Israel).

2. Abraham's Spiritual Seed: Christ and His offspring (believers/the Church).

Highly recommended if you're struggling with questions about infant baptism or Dispensationalism.

John Reisinger, *Tablets of Stone and the History of Redemption*, Revised Edition, (Frederick, MD: New Covenant Media, 2004).

The Ten Commandments...

1) are also called in Scripture "the tablets of the covenant" (Deut. 9:9, 11, 15; Heb. 9:4), "the words of the covenant" (Ex. 34:28), and "the covenant" (Deut. 4:13; 1 Kings 8:21; 2 Chr. 6:11).

2) ARE the Mosaic covenant (foundational) document (Ex. 34:28; Deut. 4:13; 1 Kings 8:21; 2 Chr. 6:11).

3) are a conditional, works covenant (Ex. 19:5-6; Deut. 7:12, 28:9).

4) were given only to the nation of Israel, not the Gentiles (Ex. 34:27-28; Deut. 5:1-3; 1 Kings 8:9; Ps. 147:19-20).

5) as a covenant had a historical beginning and end (Rom. 5:13, 20; Gal. 3:19, 25).

6) were signified by the 7th day Sabbath as the sign of the Mosaic covenant (Ex. 31:13, 16-17; Ezek. 20:11-12, 19-20).

7) were an integral part of Israel's ceremonial, priestly, sacrificial, temple worship system (Heb. 8:13-9:4ff.)

The definitive study on the nature and function of the Ten Commandments in redemptive history. The Ten Commandments are "the covenant," not the "moral law of God."

Christians' duty to obey could have been emphasized more clearly as all commands located in the New Testament. Strongest recommendation to help understand the relationship between the old and the new. If you read only one book, this is the one!

Leonard Verduin, *The Reformers and Their Stepchildren,* (Sarasota, FL: Christian Hymnary Publishers, 1991).

The Reformers persecuted the Anabaptists for believing in:

1) Believers' baptism and church membership.
2) Church discipline.
3) Non-state regulated churches (anti-theocracy).

Many 16th-century, Reformed churches were characterized by members who were doctrinally sound yet, unregenerate, hypocritical, and worldly. Evangelical, Anabaptist churches were generally more mature in godly, holy living than the Reformed churches.

Paul R. Williamson, "Covenant: The Beginning of a Biblical Idea," in *Reformed Theological Review*, Vol. 65:1, April, 2006, pp.1-14.

The author proves that God could not possibly have made a covenant of works with Adam at creation, because Divine – human covenants (not between 2 humans) confirm existing relationships, rather than establish new relationships…

"For most Reformed theologians…Covenant is seen as framing or establishing such a relationship. This, however, is not in fact what the biblical text suggests. Rather than establishing or framing such a divine-human relationship, a covenant seals or formalizes it. The biblical order is relationship, then covenant,

rather than covenant, hence relationship. Leaving aside
creation for a moment, just consider the subsequent examples
of divine-human relationships that are subsequently sealed by a
covenant:

God was clearly in relationship with Abraham from Genesis
12, yet it is not until Genesis 15 that God formalizes that
relationship by means of a covenant. Similarly, God was in a
relationship with Israel before the covenant He established
with them on Mount Sinai. Likewise, God was in relationship
with David long before he sealed that relationship by covenant
in 2 Samuel 7. And a straightforward reading of Genesis 6
suggests that God was in relationship with Noah before sealing
that relationship by covenant immediately after the Flood.

Thus the question is not whether a relationship existed between
God and creation or between God and humanity prior to the
Fall. Of course such a relationship existed. But was it a
covenant relationship? The biblical text suggest otherwise. A
covenant was a means of sealing or formalizing such a
relationship; it did not establish it. As Waltke puts it, 'A
covenant solemnizes and confirms a social relationship already
in existence.'"

Jon Zens, *Is There a Covenant of Grace?*, Searching Together,
searchingtogether.org/articles/zens/covenant.htm

"Covenant" in Scripture never refers to a prehistoric agreement
("covenant of redemption"), but always to an agreement made
in history. And, the Bible speaks of "covenants" plural (Eph
2:12; Rom. 9:4; Gal. 4:24), not "one covenant of grace." The
Holy Spirit-breathed terminology for unifying biblical history
is "purpose," (Eph. 1:5, 9, 11, 3:11) and "will" (Eph. 1:9), not
"covenant of grace."

Scripture Index

21:4 45, 47
22:17, 21 125
23:23 83
24:42-44 131
26:54 45, 47
26:56 45, 47, 142
27:9 45, 47, 142
28:1 33, 104
28:19 121, 123
28:19-20 110, 125
28:20 50, 103, 108, 119, 130

Mark
12:28-31 83
16:2 33, 104
16:9 33, 104

Luke
2:23 43
4:21 142
6:20 - 7:1 50
6:46-47 45
6:47, 49 50
7:1 50
10:26 43
16:17 51
16:18 112
18:1 103
18:31 142
21:22 142
22:19 123
22:19-20 27
24:1 33, 104
24:17, 44-47 130
24:44 45, 46, 142

John
1:16 109
1:17 100
5:39, 46 129

8:17 43
10:34 43
12:48 19
13:15 131
13:34 127, 131
14:15 103, 110, 113, 130
14:21 110, 113
14:21-24 103
15:10 103, 110, 113
15:12-13 131
15:25 43
16:23-24 126
17:12 142
17:23 7
18:32 142
19:24 142
19:28 142
19:36 142
20:1 33, 105
20:19 33, 105

Acts
1:2 110, 119
1:16 142
2:21 141
2:25-28 141
2:34-35 141
3:18 142
7:8 26, 27
8:20 137
8:32-35 141
12:22-23 17
13:14 32, 105
13:27 32, 105
13:32-41 141
13:33 142
13:42 32, 105
13:44 32, 105
15 7, 87
15:5-6 87

15:10 84, 88, 103
15:21 32, 105
15:28 84, 100
15:28-29 87
16:4 87
16:13 32, 105
17:1-2 32, 105
17:2-3 141
17:22-31 36
18:4 32, 105
18:28 141
20:7 33, 105
21:24-25 89, 100
21:25 87

Romans
1 19
1:18-32 18, 99, 138
1:18-32ff 17
1:18-2:15 14
1:24 15
2:12-14 20
2:28-29 28
3:9-20 38
3:19 43
3:19a 73
3:20 37, 38
3:20b 73
3:21 43, 70
3:26-30 72
3:31 41, 72, 138
3:31ff 86
4:1-6ff. 72
4:23-25 141
5:5 117
5:13 90, 100
5:13, 20 145
5:20 90, 100
6:2-13 128
6:4ff. 131
6:14 100

Subject Index

1689 Second London Baptist Confession of Faith 95-107

Adventism/Adventist 9, 16, 129

Anabaptists 6, 11, 146

Antinomian/Antinomianism 9, 10, 13, 14, 108, 110, 132-135

Apostolic fathers 10

Baptism (Believers' and Infant/Paedobaptism) 6, 7, 8, 58, 63, 123, 129, 144-145, 146

Covenant of Grace 65-71, 79, 96, 97, 132, 133, 138, 147

Covenant of Works 146-147

Covenant Theology 9, 13, 16, 45, 49, 59, 60, 62, 63, 65, 66, 72, 74, 75, 76, 79, 83, 84, 87, 92, 93, 95-107, 128, 129, 132-135, 138, 141, 144

Decalogue 17-40, 45, 46, 47, 50, 56, 59, 60, 61, 64, 72, 74, 75, 81, 83, 85, 88, 90-91, 100, 101, 131, 139
    See also Ten Commandments

Dispensationalism 65, 66, 79, 129, 144-145

Dominion/Reconstructionism/Theonomy 128, 133
    See also Theocracy

Evangelism 35-40, 57, 73, 125, 134, 141

Food laws (pork) 6, 7, 8, 129

Judaism 9-10

Law of Christ 11, 12, 14, 25, 37, 56, 58, 63, 64, 68, 76, 88, 90, 103-104, 110, 117, 120, 121-122, 135

Author Index

More Bible Studies by Greg Gibson at:
JesusSaidFollowMe.org

Did you find this book helpful? If so, you can see more Bible studies by Greg Gibson at: www.JesusSaidFollowMe.org, including...

"The Ex-Hypocrite" How a Big Hypocrite Received a New Life. See 6 reasons why God did not accept me (and why He may not accept you?) How God finally relieved my crippling guilt. The true confessions of an ex-hypocrite.

"The Bible's Main Message Is the Gospel About Jesus Christ Himself" Are you majoring on a minor, while minoring on THE major? Are you promoting "it" or "Him?" Beware of hobbyhorses. See 14 misdirected emphases and 36 verses.

"Calvinism, Arminianism, So What?" Understand Calvinism, Arminianism, and free will explained clearly with one chart, 23 questions, and 136 verses. Who gets the credit for your decision for Christ: The evangelist, you, or God?

"Half-Truth Hyper-Calvinism" Hyper-Calvinism refuted clearly with 3 definitions, 3 charts, 126 verses, and The 11 Points of Anti-Hyper-Calvinism. Do you talk too much about God's sovereignty? For those who talk twice as much about God's sovereignty as our responsibility.

"Big Picture Preaching" 3 Advantages of Expository Preaching From Long Passages, Instead of Short Passages. Is verse-by-verse preaching really best? Or, is theme-by-theme better? How to motivate disciples to obedience and help them grow faster.

"Why Limited Atonement Is Not Part of the Gospel" The apostles never once preached limited atonement explicitly (Calvinism's 3rd point) in their gospel messages to the lost in Acts.

"12 Questions to Ask to Find a Church" 12 questions to help you find faithful shepherds who feed Christ's sheep. Search for a church near you in 5 church directory lists.

CPSIA information can be obtained at www.ICGtesting.com
Printed in the USA
BVOW04s1759120215

387313BV00012B/415/P